GW00708658

Flash 4 for Windows

Brian Salter
and Naomi Langford-Wood

An imprint of **Pearson Education**

PEARSON EDUCATION LIMITED

Head Office:
Edinburgh Gate
Harlow
Essex CM20 2JE
Tel: +44 (0)1279 623623
Fax: +44 (0)1279 431059

London Office:
128 Long Acre
London WC2E 9AN
Tel: +44 (0)20 7447 2000
Fax: +44 (0)20 7240 5771

First published in Great Britain 2000

© Pearson Education Limited 2000

British Library Cataloguing in Publication Data
A CIP catalogue record for this book can be obtained from the British Library.

ISBN 0-13-027378-3

10 9 8 7 6 5 4 3 2

Typeset by Pantek Arts, Maidstone, Kent.
Printed and bound in Great Britain by Ashford Colour Press, Gosport, Hampshire.

Trademark notice
Flash is a trademark of Macromedia, Inc.

The publishers' policy is to use paper manufactured from sustainable forests.

Contents

●●

Introduction

Since the emergence of the World Wide Web less than a decade ago, graphic artists have demanded more and more from their software whilst also requiring fast download times for their finished masterpieces. In the past few years Macromedia's Flash has become the *de facto* standard Web design tool for creating interactive animated presentations on the Internet.

Flash is now in its fourth incarnation and works by placing sequences of images along a timeline, in much the same way as traditional cartoon artists produced acetate movies. Flash takes much of the effort out of the creation process by automating many of the tasks that traditional artists have had to do by hand, and it gives you total control over how the elements of the program interact with one another and with the end user.

Deceptively complex pages and animations can be put together in incredibly small files which download much faster than traditionally coded HTML pages. Both Netscape Navigator and Microsoft's Internet Explorer (IE) support the display of Flash files, and – in short – no serious Web developer can now afford to be without it.

■ What is in this book?

Whenever you get hold of a new program, there's always the temptation to run before you can walk. You bought Flash, after all, to get animated and interactive movies published for use on the Web or as stand-alone files. It can seem a bit tame, therefore, to have to get down to the nitty-gritty of learning how to construct simple graphics before you can make them fly; but Flash is not one of those programs that you can busk your way through – at least not if you want to release the tremendous power of the software provided.

Starting with the basics, this book takes you through the setting up of a Flash movie and explains all you need to know about the Flash environment. Very soon we're off using the drawing and painting tools and learning how to handle objects, insert text and import artwork from other programs.

The fun stuff then comes with the discovery of layers and the use of symbols and putting them to work in creating first basic and then more complex animation, coupled with interactivity and sound.

Finally, it's important to know how Flash can deliver your movies to an audience – via the Web, as stand-alone projectors or even as alternative file formats such as animated GIFs and QuickTime or AVI movie files.

Throughout the book there are copious screen shots to help you grasp what is a complex program, quickly and easily.

■ Conventions and icons

Throughout the book we have included notes, each of which is associated with an icon:

These notes provide additional information about the subject concerned.

These notes indicate a variety of shortcuts: keyboard shortcuts, 'Wizard' options, techniques reserved for experts, and so on.

These notes warn you of the risks associated with a particular action and, where necessary, show you how to avoid any pitfalls.

About the authors

Brian Salter and Naomi Langford-Wood have written a number of books on computer, business and Internet-related topics and regularly give speeches and seminars on e-commerce, the Internet and other subjects.

Brian Salter worked for many years in the BBC as a producer and presenter, and headed up communications divisions at Heathrow and Manchester Airports, Acorn Computers, Yorkshire Electricity and the Institute of Directors.

Naomi Langford-Wood's career, which has encompassed 14 directorships, began in the Midland Bank. She then worked at a senior level with a variety of companies including Bovis, Sun Life of Canada, Campbell Broking and Guinness Peat, before becoming a serial entrepreneur and moving on to the SME sector.

Both authors are directors of the Topspin Group (**http://www. topspin-group.com**) which specialises in global strategic planning, marketing, communications and all things Internet-related, including e-commerce.

1
The basics

■■

■ System requirements

Flash is a powerful authoring environment for creating animated vector graphics, and as such requires a minimum hardware configuration of:

- A Pentium 133 MHz processor running Windows 95 or 98, or NT v4
- 16 Mb of RAM or 24 Mb if running Windows NT
- 20 Mb of available disk space

Although Flash will work with such a configuration, the faster the processor and the larger the amount of available memory, the quicker and easier the software will be to work with.

Flash 4 movies can be played back on a lower-spec machine, however, allowing a wider audience to view your creations using a Web browser such as Netscape 2 or later, or Microsoft's IE3 or later, using an additional plug-in as required.

■ Software installation

To install Flash 4, insert the CD-ROM into your drive and the *autorun* feature should start off the installation process automatically (Figure 1.1).

*If autorun isn't set up to work on your computer for any reason, then simply use Windows Explorer to find the **Setup.exe** file on the CD-ROM and double-click on it, whence installation will begin.*

In common with most Windows software, you are recommended to close down any other programs that are running, and are then given a screenful of text that spells out the licence agreement.

Next, the installation software suggests that it loads the main program into your *Program Files* directory, but you can choose a new destination folder if you want to by clicking on the **Browse** button and selecting a new directory path (Figure 1.2).

Figure 1.1 The opening screen of Flash 4's installation.

Figure 1.2 You choose where you want the software to be installed.

You are now given a choice as to the type of setup you prefer. You can choose:

- Typical – which most people choose. This installs the most commonly used options.

- Compact – a minimum installation which is useful for those with little spare room on their hard disks.
- Custom – where you can choose to install the library of useful, but not essential, files; a selection of sample files; and the get-to-know-you lessons for beginners (Figure 1.3).

Figure 1.3 A choice of installation is offered.

Having chosen what you want to install, and where you want to install Flash's files, Macromedia now suggests that you install the shortcut files for the program into a start-up directory called *Macromedia Flash 4*. If you're happy with that, click **OK**, or enter a new name for the directory.

You have now given all the information that the program needs to copy across the relevant files, and after a final confirmation screen pops up (Figure 1.4) to ask if you're really, absolutely, 100% sure of your choices, installation begins.

Figure 1.4 Just checking (again) that you're happy with your choices.

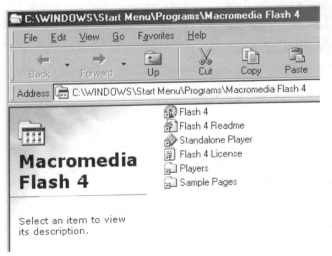

Figure 1.5 The Start Menu selection.

■■

Installation is pretty fast, even on the most basic hardware set-up. When the relevant files have been copied across, you should have a *Start:Programs* menu which has all the relevant shortcuts pertinent to your earlier selections, as well as shortcuts to sample pages and Flash players (Figure 1.5).

Now, the only thing left to do is to enter your registration details, which Flash prompts you to do before you are allowed to go any further (Figure 1.6). The FLW400 number that it asks for will be on the box in which you bought the software, as well as on your customer support card.

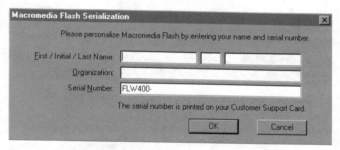

Figure 1.6 You have to enter the serial number of the software before being allowed to proceed any further.

■ Vector vs bitmap images

One of the great strengths of Flash is that it can handle vector graphics as well as bitmapped files. It is important to understand the difference between the two for a full appreciation of the power of the software.

Traditional image processing programs use bitmap graphics – also known as raster graphics. Here, each individual pixel of an image is defined and the computer is given instructions for each and every one of them.

Some file formats such as .gif and .tif files can compress these instructions where there are collections of like pixels. In effect they say to the computer something like "treat the next 51 pixels identically to this one" – or whatever.

Problems arise when you try to resize the graphic. Because pixels are a predetermined size which fit into a grid across your computer screen, resizing can give your image a ragged appearance.

Vector graphics, on the other hand, describe images as a series of mathematical formulae. These include lines and curves, as well as colours and position points. If you resize a vector graphic, its mathematical definition is altered so that the lengths of lines, or the position of certain points change; but the overall quality of the graphic is unchanged.

■ Streaming delivery

Another of the strengths of the Flash platform is its ability to stream video or audio. With traditional forms of delivering such files, the user must wait whilst the whole of the file downloads before being able to watch or listen to the file in question. Obviously, this can mean the user having to wait some time for the download, especially if it is a big file.

With streaming, on the other hand, playback starts once a portion of the file has downloaded. Whilst you watch the first portion of video, for instance, the second portion downloads and Flash feeds the frames at a specified frame rate so that the movie appears to be uninterrupted.

■ Getting to know the Flash environment

When you start up Flash in order to create and edit movies, you will work with the Editor which consists of a number of different areas with which you need to become familiar (Figure 1.7).

■■

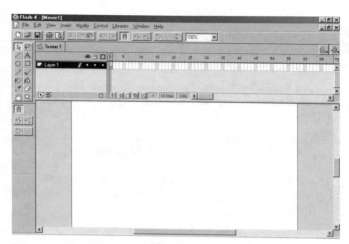

Figure 1.7 The main window of the Flash 4 Editor.

- In the top of the window is the area known as the **Timeline**. It is here that you will store the movie's frames, layers and scenes.

- Below this is the **Stage** in which you can see all the graphics that go into making up your movie.

- Situated on the left of the screen is the **Toolbox** which you use to select the tools you need in order to edit and create your various movie items.

- The grey area surrounding the Stage is a **work area** in which you can construct various graphic elements, but which does not show in the final movie.

The Timeline

You can think of a Flash movie in the same way as you would a film made for the cinema. A film is made up of a series of scenes. Each scene is made up of a sequence of frames and, just as in a real film, the individual frames play sequentially to give an impression of movement.

The Timeline is where you keep a record of the components of your movie. In it, you store information about the individual frames, and assemble all the artwork into separate layers.

 If you click inside the grey box at the top left of the Timeline (to the left of the eye in Figure 1.8) you can drag the whole of the Timeline into a new position on your screen, either to dock at one of the sides, or to float as a separate window on top of anything else on view. If you dock the Timeline horizontally (i.e. at the top or bottom of the screen) you will increase the number of easily accessible frames. If you dock it to the left or right of the screen, you will see the maximum number of layers.

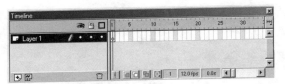

Figure 1.8 The basic Timeline.

Sometimes you will want to hide the Timeline temporarily in order to view the maximum area of stage. You can do this by choosing **Timeline** from the **View** menu or keying **Ctrl–Alt–T**.

The individual layers are used to keep your artwork separate in order for you to combine them – once they are perfected individually – into a complete movie scene. We'll investigate layers in Chapter 6.

Across the Timeline the frames are displayed with a 'ruler' of frame numbers along the top of the frames. In addition, the current frame number is shown at the bottom of the Timeline in the box to the left of the Frame Rate (shown as 12.0 fps in Figure 1.8).

The Stage

The Stage is the area in which you will 'stage' your movie. It is as big or as small as you care to make it; but the size you determine will be the size seen by your audience, and will affect the relative positions of all your movie components.

You can control both the size and appearance of the Stage by double-clicking on the Frame Rate box in the status bar of the Timeline (see Figure 1.9).

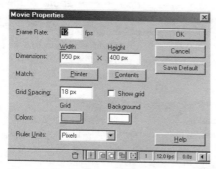

Figure 1.9 The Movie Properties dialog box is accessed by double-clicking the Frame Rate box shown at the bottom of this image.

You will see from Figure 1.9 that you have a number of options for the control of your Stage.

1. The *Frame Rate* controls at how many frames per second the movie runs. For movies viewed over the Web, 12 is a good default. Standard films normally run at 25fps.

2. The *Dimensions* of width and height are where you specify the overall size of the movie. You can specify the dimensions in inches, centimetres, pixels or points. Most people now view the Web in screen resolutions of 800×600 or 640×480 pixels, so it is best to set your dimensions smaller than this.

3. The *Ruler Units* allows you to set the unit of measurements as your default. In Figure 1.9 these are set to Pixels.

4. You can set the size of your Stage to suit the contents of the movie you are currently working on. Set *Match* by clicking on the **Contents** button, and the Stage will be sized automatically

for you. Similarly, clicking on **Printer** will set the Stage to match the printable area according to your current default printer.

5. It is often useful when aligning elements within your graphics to have a grid shown in the background. Checking the *Show Grid* box will bring up a grid which you can size with the *Grid Spacing* dialog box.

6. You can set the colours of both the grid and the background of the movie by clicking on **Grid** and **Background** and then selecting from the palette of colours that appears (Figure 1.10).

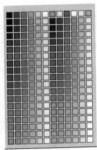

Figure 1.10 Set the Grid or Background colours from this colour dialog box.

The Toolbox

In the Toolbox are all the tools you will need to draw, select, paint and modify your artwork and objects for animation. Although the Toolbox opens to the left of your screen, you can dock it anywhere as shown in Figure 1.11.

Figure 1.11 The Toolbox docked under the main toolbar of Flash 4.

Notice that, depending upon which of the tools in the Toolbox you have chosen, a set of modifiers is displayed either at the bottom or the right-hand end of the Toolbox.

If you go to the **Windows** menu and select **Toolbar** you will be given a choice of defaults including *Show Tooltips* which pops up an icon label whenever your mouse pointer hovers over a particular icon (Figure 1.12).

Figure 1.12 Tooltips helps you select the right icon.

Rulers and Grids

We have already seen how you can use the Movie Properties dialog box to switch on the Grid control. Together with the Rulers, they are an ideal aid to draw objects with exact sizes, shapes or positions.

You can turn on the rulers by selecting **Rulers** from the **View** menu. You can also switch on the Grid from this same menu (Figure 1.13).

Figure 1.13 Turn on Rulers, Grid and other items from the View menu.

You will see that the menu allows you to snap items to the Grid. This snap feature can be set to your preferences by accessing the Snap Assistant. Simply go to the **File** menu and choose **Assistant** (Figure 1.14).

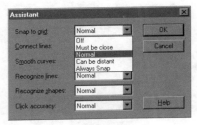

Figure 1.14 Setting your Snap options using the Assistant.

■ Testing your Flash 4 movies

As you work through creating your Flash animations you will need to play them back to check that your animations and interactive controls are working properly. There are three basic options:

1. Simple animations and interactive controls can be checked using the Controller which you access via **Window:Controller**.

2. You can test all your animations and controls by creating Flash Player movies that play within a separate window.

3. You can also publish your movie to a Web browser.

All the above are covered in detail in Chapter 12, although we will be using the checking features as we work through this book.

2 Drawing and painting

■ Creating basic shapes and objects

Although Flash lets you import drawings and shapes from other graphics programs, it also allows you to create your own drawings.

On the Toolbox you will see a number of icons offering you access to tools such as line drawing, rectangles, ovals and so on. These allow you to create both strokes and fills for a wide variety of basic shapes.

Strokes and fills are two terms that appear to have been imported from graphics programs running on Mac machines. Basically, a stroke is an outline, whilst a fill is a solid shape. By definition, since lines have no 'insides', they consist purely of strokes. But rectangles, circles and so on can have both an outline (stroke) and a fill.

The Line tool

Let's start with the Line tool. Using this, you can make simple shapes by combining a sequence of lines into, say, a star, a triangle, a pentagon, or whatever.

Figure 2.1 The Line tool with its modifiers.

You can select the Line tool from the Toolbox, or by pressing **N**. Automatically the Line modifiers appear at the end of the Toolbox. You can select the line colour by clicking on the **Line Color** box (shown as a black square in Figure 2.1). Beside this is the **Stroke Color Focus** button which enables you to assign colours to lines or strokes, as opposed to areas of fills. The **width** of the line can be set in the next box, whilst the **type** of line (solid, dashed, dotted, etc.) is chosen in the last box.

As you click and drag out a line, you will see a hairline representation of the line you are drawing which only turns into a line with all the attributes you assigned once you let go of the mouse button (Figure 2.2).

Figure 2.2 The lower line preview turns into a solid line (above) when you release the mouse.

*If you want to constrain your line to a vertical, horizontal or 45-degree angle, hold down the **Shift** key as you drag your line.*

The Oval tool

As you would expect, the Oval tool (Figure 2.3) allows you to draw ellipses and circles. You can draw them purely as outlines (strokes), as fills (solid colour), or a combination of the two. You can even fill them with gradients.

You start the oval drawing process by clicking on the appropriate tool in the Toolbox, or by keying O. If you want to draw a perfect circle, hold down the **Shift** key as you drag your outline.

Figure 2.3 The Oval tool – with modifiers similar to the Line tool.

This time the Toolbox has an extra colour box – for determining the colour of the fill.

You have the option of setting either the fill or the stroke to a 'null' colour if you want to have purely a stroke or fill colour respectively. By clicking on the appropriate colour box you will see an outline square in the top left-hand corner which tells Flash not to assign any colour to that particular selection (Figure 2.4).

*Whilst the colour palette is open for setting the stroke or the fill, you can click on the **focus** button of the fill or the stroke respectively in order to set its colour without having to first close down the present colour palette.*

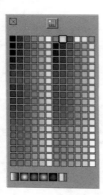

Figure 2.4 Assigning a null colour from the colour chart.

If you wish to assign an actual colour, you can simply check one of the colour boxes in the colour palette. Figure 2.5 shows a circle drawn with a dark stroke and a light fill.

Figure 2.5 A circle drawn with a dark stroke and a light fill.

You will also see, at the top centre of the colour palette, to the right of the Null Colour check box, another button that takes you to another area in which you can set colour gradients. We'll be covering this in more detail in the next chapter.

The Rectangle tool

Just as with the Oval tool, the Rectangle tool allows you to create rectangles either as outlines, fills or a combination of the two.

*You can access the Rectangle tool simply by keying **R** on your keyboard.*

This time you will see that yet another icon is introduced within the set of rectangle modifiers (Figure 2.6). The last icon allows you to determine the shape of the corners. When you click on it, a **Rectangle Settings** dialog box appears allowing you to enter any number from 0 to 999 points.

Figure 2.6 The Rectangle tool introduces yet another icon — the corner setting.

A setting of 0 will give you perfectly square corners. The higher the number entered, the rounder the corners become. In essence, what is happening is that the value that you enter is the radius in points of an imaginary circle that determines the rounded corner (see Figure 2.7).

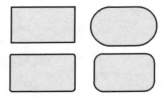

Figure 2.7 With the corner radius set to varying values, you can blunt the rectangle's corners.

The Pencil tool

When you use the Pencil tool (Figure 2.8) to create lines and curves you can ask Flash to help you smooth out the wrinkles that will almost certainly occur whether you are using a mouse cursor or a graphics tablet for your input.

 *You can enter Pencil mode by keying **P** on your keyboard.*

Figure 2.8 The Pencil tool.

You do this using the most important modifier of the Pencil tool which is the Pencil Mode, found next to the colour button (see Figure 2.9).

Figure 2.9 Modifying the accuracy of your drawing with Pencil Mode.

With it, you can set your pencil to straighten out the sketch you make so that, for instance, a rough rectangle turns into a perfect rectangle every time (Figure 2.10).

Figure 2.10 Straighten mode turns a rough sketch into a perfect rectangle.

Or a wavy line can be turned into a **smooth** curve by selecting the **Smooth** option from the Pencil Mode selector (Figure 2.11).

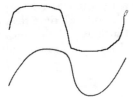

Figure 2.11 Smooth mode converts a wavy line into a smooth curve.

The degree of accuracy is set by opening up the **Assistant** from the **File** menu (see Figure 2.12) and choosing from the selections on offer:

- **Snap to grid** controls the distance before Flash snaps the line to the grid.
- **Connect lines** allows Flash to close open circles or rectangles.
- **Smooth curves** determines the degree of smoothing applied to a curve.
- **Recognize lines** determines how straight a line must be before Flash converts it to a straight line segment.
- **Recognize shapes** determines how close to a rectangle or ellipse a shape must be before Flash converts it to such an object.
- **Click accuracy** selects how close to a line segment you must be before Flash selects it.

Figure 2.12 Each area of the Assistant is selected using the drop-down menus.

If you want to avoid any of Flash's assistants without having to go to the Assistant menu to switch everything off each time, then you should choose **Ink Mode** from the Pencil Mode selections. Now when you draw a shape, every judder, twist and turn will be reproduced faithfully.

■ Painting with the Paint Bucket

We've already seen how to fill an object with colour as we create it. But what if we want to fill the object later? This is where the **Paint Bucket** tool comes into its own (Figure 2.13). Select the Paint Bucket icon (or key **U** on the keyboard). You then click the mouse cursor inside the area you wish to be filled.

Figure 2.13 The Paint Bucket tool.

Once again the colour palette is accessed by clicking on the square coloured icon in the modifiers. As well as choosing a solid colour (which, by the way, you can set as one of the 216 'safe' Web colours recognised by all Web browsers) you can set your fill as a colour gradient (Figure 2.14).

Figure 2.14 Creating a Gradient fill.

You can add up to eight separate colour gradient points by dragging the left-hand colour key into the gradient selector and changing its colour. If you want to save your new gradient definitions, click on **New**. If you want to change an existing definition, click on **Change**.

Notice also the two sliders to the right of the Gradient box. When you choose a colour by dragging the mouse around the colour palette, you can lighten or darken it by dragging the triangular arrow up or down.

If instead you wish to make one of the colours transparent, or semi-opaque, you can adjust the rectangular slide on the far right (or enter a number into the Alpha box) to determine its degree of opacity.

Once you have created your gradient, you may well wish to alter the angle and size of gradient that is applied to your selection. This is applied with the **Transform Fill** button (the last one on the right in Figure 2.13). You can use the top (square) handle to resize horizontally; the middle (round) handle to resize in all directions; and the lower (round) handle to rotate the direction of fill (Figure 2.15).

Figure 2.15 The size and angle of fill can be altered by dragging the modifier handles.

Sometimes a shape you have created is not completely enclosed. Once again Flash comes to the rescue by making an intelligent guess as to whether you meant the shape to be enclosed or not. The **Gap Size** icon (shown third from the right in Figure 2.13) offers you a choice of 'closing' small, medium or large gaps (Figure 2.16).

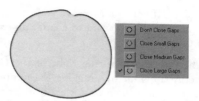

Figure 2.16 By asking Flash to close gaps for you, you can 'fill' an open shape.

Painting with the Brush tool

Flash 4's Brush tool is used for creating flows of colour – fills with no outline, if you like. You can set the shape and size of the brush by clicking on the second and third icons respectively from the right, as shown in Figure 2.17.

Figure 2.17 The Paint Brush tool.

To the left of the colour square you will see an icon representing Brush Mode, which offers you various ways to interact with lines and shapes already on the Stage (see Figure 2.18).

Figure 2.18 The Brush Mode selector options.

Depending on the mode selected, the paint used by your Brush will affect or ignore particular areas of the Stage (Figure 2.19).

- **Paint Normal** paints over lines and fills, as long as they are on the same layer. (We'll cover layers in Chapter 6.)

- **Paint Fills** paints fills and empty areas, but does not paint over lines.

- **Paint Behind** paints only blank areas of the stage, leaving lines and fills unaffected.

- **Paint Selection** paints only over a selected fill. (We'll cover selections in the next chapter.)

- **Paint Inside** paints the fill area in which you start painting, but does not cross lines.

Figure 2.19 The Painting Modes — Original Image, Paint Normal, Paint Fills, Paint Behind, Paint Selection, Paint Inside.

In a similar way to the Pencil tool, if you hold down the **Shift** key whilst dragging a line, it forces it to go either horizontally or vertically.

■ The Eraser tool

Just as you can paint using the Paint Brush, so you can erase items from your Stage using the Eraser. You can select whether you want your eraser round or square, and in one of five sizes (Figure 2.20).

Figure 2.20 The Eraser tool with modifiers.

You can erase in one of two ways:

1. By dragging using the settings offered in the Eraser Mode dialog box. The size and shape of the eraser is set using the drop-down menu shown at the far right of Figure 2.20.

2. By using the Faucet tool (which looks like a dripping tap icon).

With the former, you are offered a menu similar to the Paint Brush menu allowing you to determine whether you want to erase fills, lines, selected fills or whatever (Figure 2.21).

Figure 2.21 The Eraser Mode menu selections.

When you use the Faucet tool, you click on the line or filled area that you want to delete. The little drip at the end of the tap marks the point at which your selections are made, but with one click you can erase an entire line or filled shape, regardless of how many segments go into making up the strokes.

■ The Ink Bottle tool

You can apply an outline – a stroke – to an area of fill colour by using the Ink Bottle tool (Figure 2.22).

Figure 2.22 The Ink Bottle tool with modifiers.

Having selected the colour, width and style, you apply the Ink Bottle to an area as shown in Figure 2.23.

Figure 2.23 The Ink Bottle paints a stroke round an area of fill.

3
Objects

So far, we've concentrated – naturally enough – on creating objects. But it won't be long before you will want to alter your creations in some way.

Modifying objects is an all-encompassing term. It can include:

- moving
- colouring/re-colouring
- straightening
- smoothing
- scaling
- rotating ...
- ... and a whole lot more besides!

■ Selecting objects

The first step in changing an object is to select it, and Flash 4 offers a variety of ways in which you can do this.

In common with most image processing programs, you can use the arrow tool to click on an object in order to select it, but you can also select items by fully enclosing them – either using a rectangular selector or a freeform lasso.

We'll come to these methods in a moment. But because of the complex nature of many of the shapes you will be creating, it is necessary at this point to understand the way in which Flash 4 allows you to add to – or subtract from – your selections.

If you go to your **File** menu and select **Preferences**, you will see a dialog box like the one shown in Figure 3.1.

The penultimate check box allows you to set your selection options – either in *Shift Select* mode, or in *Additive mode*. With the former (which is the default) you hold the **Shift** key down as you make a selection to add it to the items you have already selected. With the latter, anything you select is automatically added to your current selection.

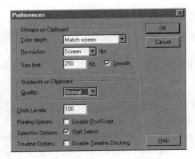

Figure 3.1 You set your select options from here.

Let's make some selections.

Selecting with the Arrow tool

The first thing to understand is that what you may regard as a straightforward and simple shape, is not necessarily the way that Flash 4 treats it. Every time there is a twist or turn in a seemingly simple line, Flash defines a new vector path that then counts as a separate part of that line.

If, for instance, we draw a rectangle with rounded corners, Flash will treat it as four straight lines and four corners. In other words a rectangle will be made up of eight vectors.

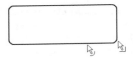

Figure 3.2 Hovering your cursor over a segment will show you what type it is.

Select the **Arrow** tool from the toolbar and move your mouse over your intended selection (Figure 3.2). The cursor will change into either a curve point or a corner point. By simply clicking on a segment, you can select it and the segment will become highlighted. At this point, the cursor then changes once again – as you can see in Figure 3.3.

Figure 3.3 A selected segment with its associated cursor.

Remember, that to add another segment to your selection you either need to **Shift** select it, or set your preferences as discussed above. But if you want to select the entire shape, try double-clicking it instead. As long as all the segments are touching one another, the entire shape should become selected.

 *If you are using another tool and you want to quickly select the Arrow tool, press the **Ctrl** key. The Arrow tool will remain your default as long as the **Ctrl** key is held down.*

You can select a filled area in the same way you would select a line. With the Arrow tool you just click on it. The cursor changes into a selection arrow and the fill changes to a contrasting checkerboard pattern (Figure 3.4).

Figure 3.4 Clicking the fill (left) creates a checkerboard pattern (right).

If you want to select a group of objects – lines, corners, fills etc. – the quickest method is to use the Arrow tool to drag a rectangle over the objects to be selected. Releasing the mouse selects everything lying inside the rectangle.

 *If you want to select everything on the Stage, you can go to the **Edit** menu and choose **Select All**. Or an even quicker method is to key **Ctrl-A**.*

Selecting with the Lasso tool

Using the Arrow tool and drawing out rectangles is a good way of selecting objects if there is enough room between them; but if objects are close together, a safer way of selecting them is to use the **Lasso** tool, which works in a similar way to most other image processing programs.

From the toolbar, select the Lasso tool (the one next to the Arrow tool) or simply press L on the keyboard. Holding the mouse key down, drag a freeform selection around the objects you wish to select and let go. Whatever is enclosed by the lasso will become selected.

You don't need to close the lasso selection if you are sure that the line that would have been drawn from your end point to your start point fully encloses your intended selection.

For selecting really complex shapes it can prove difficult to hold the mouse key down and drag all round the objects. Instead, Flash offers you a method which will be kinder on your hand muscles! When you select the Lasso tool, you will see a set of modifier icons, one of which is the **Polygon mode** icon (Figure 3.5).

Figure 3.5 The Polygon mode icon is the one on the right.

If you select this before making your selection you will find that you can click your way around a shape adding segments as you go along. To close the selection process, double-click your mouse. You can even combine the two lasso operations by temporarily holding down the **Alt** key whilst using the Lasso, whence you will be taken to Polygon mode for as long as you hold down the **Alt**.

Selecting portions

There are times when you will want to select only part of an element, and this is done using the Arrow or Lasso tools to enclose the areas in which you are interested (see Figure 3.6)

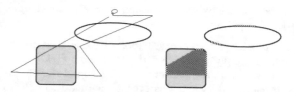

Figure 3.6 Selecting over the objects (left) creates a partial selection (right).

Deselecting parts of a selection

We've seen how you can select objects in a variety of ways in Flash 4. Deselecting an object is much simpler. All you need to do is use the Arrow tool and **Shift** click the partial selection.

To deselect everything you can:

1. Go the **Edit** menu and choose **Deselect All**.
2. Key **Shift + Ctrl-A**
3. Click in an empty area of your Stage.

So now that we've seen how to select and deselect items on our Stage, the next question is: what can we do with our selections?

■ Repositioning objects

Once you have drawn an object, the chances are that you will want to position it accurately to line up with other items on your Stage.

The quickest (and crudest) method is to click on the object with your arrow key and drag it to a new position. To help you position your object more accurately, you might care to switch on the rulers by going to your **View** menu and selecting **Rulers**. You could also switch on the positioning grid with **View:Grid**.

For more accuracy you could select the Arrow key and click on the object, and then use your four cursor keys to move the object horizontally or vertically, one pixel at a time. (If you hold down the **Shift** key as you do this, the object will move eight pixels at a time.)

If you want to specify exactly where your item should go you can instead use the **Object Inspector**. Go to the **Window** menu and select **Inspectors:Object** in order to open a window similar to that shown in Figure 3.7.

Figure 3.7 Using the Object Inspector to reposition your object.

Here you can see that it is a simple matter of entering x and y co-ordinates for accurate placement of your object. The co-ordinate points refer to the top left-hand corner of the object's bounding box; but you can, if you wish, check the box in the Object Inspector to specify using the centre point of the object.

■ Simple editing commands

In common with most Windows programs, Flash supports the standard copy, cut and paste options. It also has a couple of aces up its sleeve to simplify the process further.

To delete a selection, select the elements you want to delete and press the **Delete** key (or go to the **Edit** menu and choose **Clear**). Flash removes your selection.

To cut a selection, select the elements and key **Ctrl-X** (or **Edit:Cut**). The selection is copied to the Clipboard and removed from the Stage.

To copy a selection, select the elements and key **Ctrl-C** (or **Edit:Copy**). The selection is copied to the Clipboard.

To paste the Clipboard contents to the centre of your current view, press **Ctrl-V** (**Edit:Paste**).

Sometimes it will be important to paste the clipboard contents in their original location – when you are creating multi-layered objects and exact positioning on another layer is crucial, for instance. For this version of pasting, key **Ctrl-Shift-V** or from your **Edit** menu select **Paste in Place**.

You can duplicate an object by keying **Ctrl-D** (or using **Edit:Duplicate**). Although this doesn't change the contents of the Clipboard, it duplicates the original – offset – so that you can see both the original and the duplicate (Figure 3.8).

Figure 3.8 Duplicating a rectangle offsets the copy and selects it by default.

*Instead of using **Copy** and **Paste**, you can instead hold the **Ctrl** key down whilst dragging an object. A new copy of the item appears with the original left intact.*

There is one more Paste command – **Paste Special** – that we'll be looking at in Chapter 5 which allows you to paste in objects from other programs. This allows you to edit the object in another program and immediately translate those changes to the object in Flash.

■ Changing line segments

Once drawn, you can use the Arrow tool to grab and reposition the end points of a straight line or curve. This allows you to lengthen or shorten them until they accurately reflect what you want.

Flash also allows you to change the direction of a line segment by dragging the end of the line to a new position, or to change the direction of the end of a curve by dragging its end in a similar manner.

You can also change the shape of a curve, or turn a straight line into a curve by grabbing a segment in the middle of a run and dragging it to a new position. Flash automatically redraws the curve (Figure 3.9).

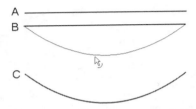

Figure 3.9 Dragging the centre of a straight line (A) until you get the outline you want (B) creates a curve (C).

If you want to create a new corner point, rather than a curve, repeat the above, but hold down the **Ctrl** key as you do it. The shape of the new curve will depend on the shape you started with, but with a little practice you will soon see what a powerful feature this is (Figure 3.10).

Figure 3.10 Ctrl dragging produces new corner points.

■ Reshaping filled areas

Just as you can change the shapes of lines and curves, so too can you change the shape of a filled area. Although you can't see the edges of fills, unless they have a stroked outline, they do nevertheless have their own (invisible) outlines. This means that you can select their curve points or corner points and distort them just as you would a stroked outline (Figure 3.11)

Figure 3.11 Here a circular fill has had its lower half dragged out and the upper segment is being given a new corner point drag.

■ Resizing objects

Flash 4 enables you to resize an object in one of four ways:

1. You can use the **Arrow** tool to drag out the dimensions.
2. You can apply a **Scale** command.
3. New dimensions can be entered into the **Object Inspector**.
4. You can use the **Transform Inspector**.

1. With your object selected, click on the Resize icon (Figure 3.12) in order to give your selection some resizing handles.

Figure 3.12 The Resize icon.

By dragging out the central handles, you can resize either horizontally (Figure 3.13) or vertically. Dragging one of the corner handles, on the other hand, resizes in both directions so
that your aspect ratio remains the same.

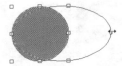

Figure 3.13 Resizing horizontally.

2. To resize an object using the Scale command, go to the
   Modify menu and choose **Transform:Scale and Rotate** (Figure
   3.14). If you add a percentage greater than 100%, the object
   will be uniformly magnified. To reduce its size, however, enter
   a number less than 100%.

Figure 3.14 Using the Scale and Rotate menu.

3. When we considered repositioning an object earlier on, we
   saw that one can use the **Object Inspector** to enter co-
   ordinates (see Figure 3.7). You can use this same tool to enter
   width and height settings – remembering that if you want to
   scale an object proportionally then this is not the tool for you!
   Each setting has to be entered by you; so if you want auto-
   matic scaling, use the **Transform Inspector**.

4. You can access the **Transform Inspector** by going to the
   Windows menu and choosing **Inspectors:Transform**. Having
   selected your object, you need to tick the check box labelled
   Uniform if you want your object resized proportionally and then
   enter the percentage increase or decrease in the **Scale** boxes.

Click on **Apply** to make the changes, or on **Copy** if you want to make the changes to a copy of the original (see Figure 3.15)

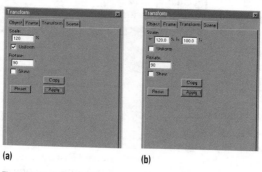

(a)   (b)

Figure 3.15 Using the Transform Inspector to resize (a) proportionally and (b) dis-proportionally.

If you want to resize several objects at once, make your selections first and then use any of the above four methods to convert them as one batch.

■ Changing an object's orientation

In common with most imaging programs, Flash 4 allows you to **flip, skew,** or **rotate** an object, but once again the software comes up with a variety of ways in which you can do so. The quickest (and crudest) way is to use the **rotate** icon on your toolbar and then to use the 'handles' attached to your selection outines to either rotate or skew the object. In Figure 3.16, for instance, an object (A) is selected (B) and the Rotate icon selected, which produces an outline with 'handles' (C). Dragging one of the corner handles rotates the object (D), whilst grabbing one of the centre handles skews the object (E).

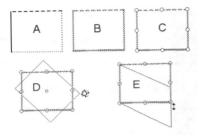

Figure 3.16 Rotating and skewing using the object's rotation handles.

If, instead of using the Rotate icon, you use the Scale icon next to it, you can *flip* the object – either horizontally or vertically – by grabbing one of the resulting handles and dragging it right out to the other side of the bounding box. The flipped object starts small, but grows as you continue to drag away from the bounding box.

You can rotate objects easily, either in 90° steps (from the **Modify** menu choose **Transform:Rotate Left** – or **Right**) or by specified amounts by selecting **Modify:Transform:Scale and Rotate** whence a dialog box as in Figure 3.14 appears and you can just enter the degree of rotation.

Similarly you can use the **Transform Inspector** that we saw in Figure 3.15 to set the amount of skew.

■ Alignment of objects

When we move on to animation techniques in Chapter 8 it will become apparent just how important it is to be able to align individual items together on the Stage. Flash 4 allows you to align selected objects along their tops, bottoms, sides, or even by their centres.

You can even resize one object to match the dimensions of another so that they are all the same width or height.

You access the Alignment dialog box (Figure 3.17) by going to the **Modify** menu and choosing **Align** or keying **Ctrl-K** instead.

Figure 3.17 The Alignment dialog box.

As you can see in Figure 3.17, the default setting is to have vertical and horizontal alignment, as well as size matching, switched off. Having selected the objects you want aligned, you can choose to align them vertically or horizontally via their midpoints or by either edge, as well as determining the spacing between each. The icons within the Alignment dialog box show you what is on offer.

Similarly, the **Match Size** option allows you to match objects horizontally, vertically or proportionally with one another.

▪ Grouping objects together

As you work with a number of objects on your Stage, the time will come when you will want to regard groups of individual objects as a single object in their own right. Flash allows you to group these selected objects together by going to the **Modify menu** and selecting **Group**.

Once grouped, they behave like any other single object, except that the group that you last created will be given priority in terms of appearing at the top of the 'stack' of visible objects. In other words, if you have two groups of objects which overlap, the one that was last created will appear on top of the older group.

*You can change the visibility order by simply selecting **Modify: Arrange:Send to Back** (or **Bring to Front**) so that different grouped elements have priority.*

If, having created a group, you wish to make changes to one element within the group, you can edit it by double-clicking on the grouped item, whence a flag appears in the top left corner of the stage informing you that you are no longer editing directly on to the Stage, but instead within the group only (Figure 3.18).

Figure 3.18 The Group 'flag' shows you are no longer editing the Scene.

When you have finished making changes to your grouped item, click once again on the **Scene** 'flag' to the left of the Group 'flag' to return to normal editing mode.

4 Type

Inserting text

Setting type attributes

Converting type to objects

■ Inserting text

As well as placing objects on your Stage, you will almost certainly want to use text in one form or another within your Flash environment. The Text tool – represented by a capital A – together with its modifiers, is what you will initially use for inserting text into your work.

Start by accepting the default settings offered to you, but ensure that the **Text Field** button (shown as **abl** in Figure 4.1) is *not* selected. As you move the cursor across the Stage it will turn into a crosshair with an **A** attached to it. Now, click on the Stage where you would like to enter some text and a text box will appear as shown in Figure 4.1.

Figure 4.1 The Text tool modifiers, together with text box and text tool cursor.

As you start to enter your text, you will see the text box expanding so that your words remain entirely enclosed (Figure 4.2).

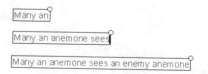

Figure 4.2 The round handle in the top right corner shows there is no word wrap switched on. Note how the text box expands to accommodate the text.

We mentioned in the previous exercise that you should make sure the text field box is left unchecked. The result was a text field on the Stage with a round handle in its upper right-hand corner. If the text field box *had* been checked, you would first have had to drag out a box on your Stage to the width that you wanted. Flash 4 would then have wrapped the text round at the right-hand end and created extra lines to accommodate your text.

Another way to have set a finite width would have been to start with an expandable box – as before – but then to have dragged the round handle to the desired width. The round handle would have turned square and a finite width would have been created (Figure 4.3).

> Can you imagine an imaginary menagerie manager imagining managing an imaginary menagerie?

Figure 4.3 The square handle shows that the width has been fixed.

There is a third type of text field box used for interactive, editable text. We'll look at this in Chapter 9.

■ Setting type attributes

Setting the weight and style of a font in Flash 4 is comparable to that in most DTP and word processing packages. You can set the attributes before you start typing text, or highlight text that you want to change in some way and then set its attributes.

Using the Text modifiers, select the font you want, together with its size, whether you want it bold and/or italic, and – using the alignment icon – whether you want it left, right, centred or fully justified. You can also set the colour of the font in this manner.

*Instead of using the modifier icons you can, if you want, access most of these settings from the **Modify:Style** menu.*

You can also set the paragraph attributes, much as you would in any word processing program. Click on the **Paragraph** modifier to bring up a dialog box (Figure 4.4) offering you the facilities of adjusting:

- left and right margins
- the amount of indentation for the first line of text
- the spacing between lines.

Figure 4.4 The Paragraph Properties dialog box.

Remember, though, that unless you show the borders of your text field in your final presentation, your audience will not be aware of the size of your margins. However, this facility may well be useful if you intend that this text should be editable in the final presentation (see Chapter 9).

 By default, Flash uses point size when determining the spacing between lines of text. However, if you enter the line spacing in centimetres, inches or pixels, Flash will convert that setting to points automatically. So if you enter, say, 2 cm by mistake, don't be surprised if you get a line spacing of 57 points!

If you want to set a number of font attributes in one go you might find it quicker and easier to go to the **Modify:Font** menu and thereby call up the font modifier dialog box, as shown in Figure 4.5. Here you can choose:

- the font you want
- its size
- to set bold and/or italic

- whether you want it set as superscript, subscript or normal script
- the amount of spacing between letters
- whether you want kerning switched on.

Kerning is a measure of how much spacing there is between letters. Certain combinations of letters – such as 'to' or 'ti' – can appear either too far apart or too close together because of the shape of the letters. When you kern a selection of letters you can alter the spacing between them to make them look better and also to aid legibility.

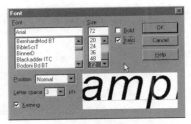

Figure 4.5 Setting multiple font attributes.

Up till now we have seen that you can set many different attributes for the fonts you are using. However, as Flash saves all the type information into the final movie, it is essential that your intended audience has the same fonts installed in order to be able to see your movie as you intended it.

You could convert your type into objects with outlines (see below), but that will take up extra file space.

Alternatively you could use the most common typefaces – Arial, Times, Courier, etc. – and hope that your audience has them loaded on their computers.

*Thirdly, you can use what Flash calls **Device Fonts**. If you look in your font list within Flash, you will see at the top of the list are three fonts called '_sans', '_serif' and '_typewriter'. If you select one of these fonts, the Flash Player will use a font on the local computer that most closely matches the original device font.*

■■■

■ Converting type to objects

We mentioned above that there will be instances when you will want to convert your text into an object in order to be able to manipulate it as you would any other object. You can only convert an entire block of text at one time; individual characters cannot be converted by themselves. Once you have converted type to line strokes and fills, you will no longer be able to edit your text.

To convert your text to an object, select it and then go to the **Insert** menu. Choose **Convert to Symbol**.

We shall be taking a closer look at symbols in Chapter 7.

5 Imported artwork

Using imported graphics in Flash

Acceptable file formats

Converting bitmaps to vector elements

Painting with a bitmapped image

Using the Magic Wand

■ Using imported graphics in Flash

As well as enabling you to produce simple graphics, Flash 4 also allows you to import graphics from other programs. This gives you the option of producing something using advanced features in another package and then using them within Flash.

When importing graphic elements, you can import both vector graphics and raster – or bitmapped – images. So if you already use image processing applications such as Freehand, Illustrator, PaintShop Pro or CorelDraw, you can rest assured that it is likely you will be able to utilise any existing artwork.

Flash 4 can also import movie files, and we'll look at this in a moment.

Be aware that, although you can import most vector graphics, you may find that not all the features of other vector-producing applications translate readily into Flash.

■ Acceptable file formats

If you want hassle-free translation from another vector program into Flash 4, the best way is to import graphics as *.swf* (Shockwave format) files. For example, Freehand (another program from the Macromedia stable) can accept most vector formats from other programs and resave them as .swf files. These files have the advantage of containing gradient and vector layers intact, whereas Flash may not cope well with gradients in other formats. You could of course always re-create the gradients using Flash's own tools, but that rather defeats the object, doesn't it?

However, not everyone has Freehand, of course. If you have Adobe Illustrator, then Flash 4 recognises 88, 3.0, 5.0, 6.0 and 7.0 formats. Although Flash can read .eps files created by Illustrator, it will have difficulty with .eps files created by other applications.

Other file types that are supported are metafile types such as .emf (enhanced metafile) and .wmf (Windows metafile), both of which can contain vector and raster information, and bitmapped types such as .bmp (Windows bitmap), .gif (Compuserve graphic image format – including animated GIF), .jpg (JPEG) and .png (Portable Network Graphics).

Flash can also handle QuickTime movies (.mov) and AutoCAD's DXF (.dxf) format.

Importing raster graphics

Raster (bitmapped) graphics can easily be brought into the Flash environment by going to the **File** menu and selecting **Import**, whence an **Import** dialog box (as in Figure 5.1) appears.

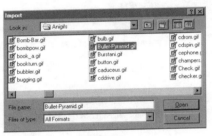

Figure 5.1 The Import dialog box.

You navigate in the normal way to the file on your computer system and either click on **Open**, or double-click on the file in question.

Flash responds by both storing a copy of the bitmap in question on the Stage in whatever layer is currently active (see Chapter 6) as well as placing a copy of it in its library (see Chapter 7).

Sometimes you will want to import a number of sequential files for use as keyframes in a movie. (We'll cover keyframes in Chapter 8.) If all the file names are identical, apart from a series of sequential numbers, then Flash will ask you if you want to import all, rather than just one, image (Figure 5.2).

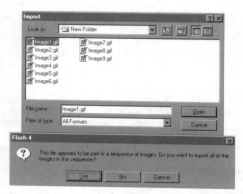

Figure 5.2 Flash recognises that Image1 is one of a sequence of files, and offers to import them all for you.

Importing vector-based graphics

Importing vector graphics is a very similar process to that used for raster graphics. The main difference lies in what Flash does with the file.

Whereas a bitmapped image is placed on the Stage as well as in the Library, a vector image is placed on the Stage as a grouped object but it is not placed in the Library. You can *ungroup* the vector image (by choosing **Modify:Ungroup**) allowing you to work with the ungrouped object as you would with any vector image created within Flash itself.

When importing vector files in Adobe's Illustrator format, the original layers are recreated within Flash.

Importing via the Clipboard

Both bitmaps and vector images can be pasted into Flash via the Windows Clipboard. It's a little bit hit-and-miss, however, as vector objects in particular can lose some of their information, leading to oddities in the translation. But as a 'quick and dirty' method it is very simple.

Start by opening up the application used to create the graphic and select and copy the object (usually, though not always, using **Ctrl-C**). Open up Flash (if it is not already open) or click anywhere within the Flash environment to 'bring it alive' and click **Ctrl-V** or **Edit:Paste**.

Once again, if the object is a bitmapped image, it will be placed both on the Stage and in the Library, whilst if it is a vector image it will be placed only on the Stage.

Flash also has an import option which is known as *Paste Special*. This differs from the previous use of the Clipboard in that, instead of pasting the contents directly on to the Stage, Flash pastes them at the same time as creating links to the original files. If you want to modify these items, Flash will then open up the original program where you can make your changes; anything that you then change will be reflected back in the image on Flash's Stage.

Figure 5.3 The Paste Special dialog box which changes depending on what is in the Clipboard.

In Figure 5.3 you can see that you are sometimes given the option as to which format you would like to paste your file. For example, graphic elements on this occasion can be pasted as metafiles or bitmapped files.

■ Converting bitmaps to vector elements

You can convert a bitmapped image into a vector file allowing
you to work on the image in exactly the same way you would
any other vector object. Because photographic-type images could
well end up with a massive number of colour shadings and vector curves, it is necessary to strike a balance between accuracy
and file manageability.

With the bitmapped image on your Stage, select **Modify:Trace
Bitmap** from the file menu and a dialog box similar to that
shown in Figure 5.4 will appear.

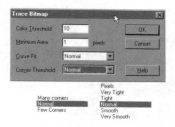

Figure 5.4 The Trace Bitmap dialog box with Corner Threshold and Curve Fit options.

As you can see, there are a number of parameters you can enter
and they control how close a match your final vector image will
be to the original bitmapped image.

- **Color Threshold** determines the amount of similar colours
  that are clumped together within one vector object. With a
  low threshold, more individual colours are recognised, but
  the downside to this is that you end up with many more vector objects and a correspondingly larger file size.

- **Minimum Area** guides Flash into working with neighbouring
  pixels to work out a colour match. The more pixels it works
  with, the lower the detail and the lower the file size.

- **Curve Fit** determines the smoothness of the curved outlines
  around individual vector shapes.

- **Corner Threshold** guides Flash in creating sharp corners or more rounded ones.

Although Macromedia recommends that settings for photographs should be 'Color Threshold, 10; Minimum Area, 1; Curve Fit, pixels; Corner Threshold, Many corners', you are likely to end up with huge files if you follow this advice (see Figures 5.5 and 5.6). Ask yourself why you would want to have this level of resolution in your vector object and see if you cannot find a way around it – perhaps by combining a vector and a bitmapped graphic so that only the area that needs to be vectorised is converted.

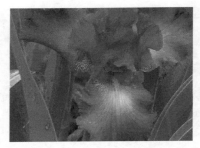

Figure 5.5 A picture of some irises, traced with a Color Threshold of 10 and a Minimum Area of 1.

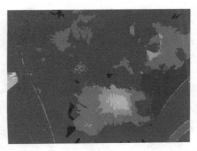

Figure 5.6 The same picture traced with a Color Threshold of 20 and a Minimum Area of 10.

■ Painting with a bitmapped image

Bitmapped images can be used to fill other areas as a repeating pattern. You might find this useful if, for instance, you wanted to fill some text with an image pattern, or wanted to 'paint' the pattern on to the side of an object.

First select the bitmapped image on your Stage (Figure 5.7).

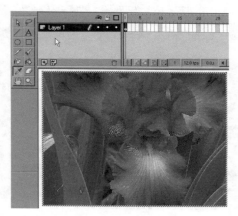

Figure 5.7 First we select the bitmap.

From the **Modify** menu select **Break Apart**. You will see that the entire bitmapped image looks as if it is covered by a tiny grid, similar to that shown in Figure 5.8.

If you now select the Dropper tool and click anywhere on the broken apart image it will select it as a fill pattern so that it can be used in a similar way to a gradient fill.

You will see that the Paint Bucket tool has been selected (Figure 5.9), and that the Fill Colour icon in the modifier palette is filled with a tiny representation of the image. You could use this image to fill a selected area of an object. Alternatively you could try using the Paint Brush or create filled rectangles and ellipses to see the power of the software in action (see Figure 5.10).

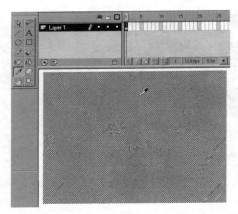

Figure 5.8 The bitmap is 'broken apart' waiting for the Dropper tool.

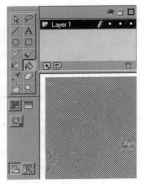

Figure 5.9 The Dropper tool is replaced by the Paint Bucket and the fill colour is replaced by the image.

Once you have filled your object, you might decide that you want the focus of the fill altered. Perhaps you want another part of the fill as the focus, or you want it resized.

Figure 5.10 Filling and painting areas with our original image.

To move the centre of a bitmapped fill, select the Paint Bucket tool and then choose the **transform fill** modifier (the bottom right icon shown in figure 5.9). If you position the resulting cursor over your fill object and click, you will see handles for manipulating the object appear. You use

- the central handle to reposition the centre of the fill;
- the bottom or top handle to alter the height of the fill;
- the side handles to alter its width;
- the bottom left corner handle to alter the size proportionally;
- the top right corner handle to rotate the object.

If you alter the fill pattern and are likely to want to use these settings again, select the modified fill and choose Insert:Convert to Symbol. You can then use this symbol (see Chapter 7) again and again.

■ Using the Magic Wand

You can use the Magic Wand tool to select areas of a bitmapped image that have like colours. For instance, on the picture of the iris that we have been using we might want to select a leaf.

First you need to select the bitmapped image as before and break it into its component colours (**Modify:Break Apart**). Unselect the image.

Now choose the Lasso tool and select the **Magic Wand** modifier. By clicking on particular colours of the image with your Magic Wand you can select whole areas of like colour.

 You can alter the Magic Wand's settings by clicking on the right-hand modifer. Here you can set the threshold and the smoothing levels as before.

If you want to, you can then modify that particular area – such as painting it with solid colour using the bucket fill (see Figure 5.11).

Figure 5.11 Using the Magic Wand you can select an area (left) and paint it with a solid colour (right).

6 Layers

Layers

Using the Layers dialog box

Using the Timeline to control layers

Stacking objects on different layers

Guide layers

Mask layers

Paste in place

■ Layers

Importing and creating artwork in Flash is all very well, but very quickly you could get to the stage where the workings on one section of your artwork could interfere with other aspects of your image creation. In addition, the more images that are stacked one on top of the other, the more complicated the manipulating of those images becomes.

Flash – in common with many other image creation programs – uses **Layers** to circumvent this problem. Think of a pad made up of a number of sheets of tracing paper; but instead of being translucent, you can see clearly through each one. Each different sheet has a separate part of the image you are working on and you can arrange for separate sheets to hide or display the work underneath their own. You can move the layers around in any order and you can move the objects within each layer.

The main power of layers lies in the fact that you can edit or manipulate the objects on a particular layer without affecting any of the objects on other layers; you can also get the objects on one particular layer to affect the objects on another layer in some predetermined way.

When it comes to animating your movie, layers really come into their own by providing the facility to move objects along pre-defined paths. We'll deal with animations in Chapter 8.

Flash gives a visual representation of each layer at the start of the Timeline. When you start up Flash there will, of course, be only one layer since you have yet to create any. You can see in Figure 6.1 that there is a selection of icons associated with the layer Timeline. We'll come to the use of the top three icons in a short while. For the moment, though, you will notice two icons in the bottom left-hand corner which are used for creating *new layers* and *new guide layers* respectively. On the bottom right-hand side is a dustbin (or trashcan) icon used for *deleting* layers.

Figure 6.1 Flash begins with one layer.

You will also see that, by default, Flash has called your base layer 'Layer 1'. As each new layer is created, it will be given a number equivalent to the amount of new layers created (not necessarily the number of layers in existence, since you might have deleted or merged some).

You can easily rename these layers and, in fact, it is probably best to do so since as you create more and more layers it is easy to lose track of where you are. To rename a layer, simply double-click on the name and type in a new one.

There is another way to rename your layer, and that is via the **Layer Properties** dialog box. We'll be returning to this dialog box throughout this chapter. To access it, go to your **Modify** menu and click on **Layer**, or else right-click on the layer itself and choose **Properties**. The dialog box will be similar to that shown in Figure 6.2.

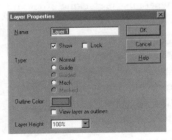

Figure 6.2 The Layer Properties dialog box.

The first field is where you can type in a name for the layer. In fact, when the box appears, you will see the name is already highlighted, waiting for you to type in your new name straight away.

Creating and deleting layers

It is normal to create layers as you need them, although there is no reason why you could not create a number of layers to start off with and then work on them individually after that.

You can create layers in a number of ways. The simplest is to click on the + icon at the bottom left of the Timeline that we saw in Figure 6.1. However, you could also **Insert** a **Layer** from the menu bar (Figure 6.3) or even key **Alt-I** then **Alt-L**.

Figure 6.3 Inserting a new layer via the menu bar.

Flash will always create a new layer above the currently selected layer, so it is important to think where in the stacking order you want your new layer to appear.

Which is the current layer? If you look at Figure 6.1 you will see that Layer 1 has a black background, as well as having a Pencil icon. (We'll return to that pencil in a moment.) All the layers that are not the currently selected one will have a blue or grey background.

Deleting a layer is just as easy. Either select the layer by clicking on it and then drag it to the dustbin or just click on the dustbin with the layer selected.

Alternatively, right-click on the layer itself and select **Delete Layer**.

*If you want to delete more than one layer at a time, make a selection of layers together holding down the **Ctrl** key as you do so, and then click on the dustbin.*

■ Using the Layers dialog box

We saw in Figure 6.2 that you can use the Layers dialog box to rename a particular layer. It can also be used to set other parameters for that layer.

Visibility

For instance, when you have objects on many layers, it sometimes gets confusing to have all the layers visible on the Stage at once when trying to tweak one small aspect of a particular object. To aid you in your editing, you can make any of the layers temporarily invisible so that they don't get in the way of the object you are trying to see.

You will see in figure 6.2 that the second row has two tick boxes. If the **Show** box has a tick then the layer will be visible; no tick and the layer will become invisible.

Locking

Similarly, once you have worked on an object you may wish to protect it from accidental changes made when editing another object. In this instance, if you tick the **Lock** box, it will protect that layer from any further changes. When the layer is locked, you can still see the objects, but you cannot select them or edit them.

Outline colours

One of the options allows you to view the contents of a layer as a set of outlines and to change the outline colour. In order to aid the placing of objects on the Stage relative to one another, Flash gives you the option of displaying only the outlines of objects. To do so, tick the check box marked **View Layer as Outlines**.

So that you can determine which outlines are on which layers, you can colour-code the outlines so that, for instance, the outlines of objects on Layer 1 could be in red, Layer 2 in green, and so on.

Clicking on the coloured rectangle next to **Outline Color** will bring up a colour palette from which you can choose whichever colour you wish (see Figure 6.4).

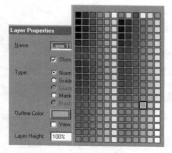

Figure 6.4 Changing the outline colours of your wire frames.

Changing a layer's height

The lowest box in the Layer Properties dialog box allows you to alter the height of the layer bars in the Timeline. This is especially useful if you want to view the waveforms of sound channels which are hard to see at the normal 100% setting (see Chapter 10).

Changing the type of layer

You will have noticed that the middle of the Layer Properties dialog box is taken up with a series of radio buttons allowing you to determine the type of layer you wish to work on.

You can set a layer as:

1. Normal
2. Guide
3. Guided
4. Mask
5. Masked

In addition, a layer can be a Motion Guide layer which we will look at in Chapter 8.

1. The **Normal** layer is the default, and all objects in a normal layer will appear in your final movie.
2. **Guide** layer objects do not appear in a final movie. They are there purely to guide objects on other layers to be positioned accurately, or to move in a particular direction or path.
3. A **Guided** layer is aligned to a guide layer and reacts according to the settings in the latter.
4. A **Mask** layer can either hide or reveal the contents of layers lying below in the stacking order.
5. These lower layers are called **Masked** layers.

In the Timeline, these different layers are shown with different label icons, as shown in Figure 6.5.

Figure 6.5 Each type of layer has its own individual icon.

■ Using the Timeline to control layers

Many of the controls we talked about in the previous section can be more easily achieved by clicking on icons in the Timeline.

If you look at Figure 6.6, you will see three icons in the top right-hand corner which are, respectively:

1. Visibility
2. Locking
3. Outlines

■■■

Figure 6.6 Control icons in the Timeline.

If you click on a bullet below the 'eye' icon, the bullet will turn into a red cross sign, and that layer will no longer be visible.

Click on a bullet below the padlock icon, and the bullet turns into a padlock. Now, any objects on that particular layer are protected from being edited.

A click on a bullet below the square icon itself turns into a square, leaving all objects in that layer shown as outlines only. The colour of the square is representative of the colour of the layer's outlines.

 If you want to change the visibility, lock or outline properties of a number of consecutive layers in one go, click a bullet on the first layer and drag the mouse button through all the other layers.

■ Stacking objects on different layers

When you place objects on different layers, those in the higher layer levels will always appear 'on top' of the lower objects.

Suppose you have three shapes – a lozenge, circle and square – placed on Layers 1, 2 and 3 respectively. As you will see in Figure 6.7, the circle is placed over the lozenge, whilst both are eclipsed by the square.

If we now grab the individual layers and drag them into a new order, as shown in Figure 6.8, you will see that the stacking order of the objects changes accordingly.

Although only one layer may be selected at any time, this does not mean you cannot edit items on other layers.

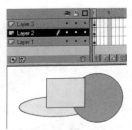

Figure 6.7 Three objects are stacked in the order of their respective layers.

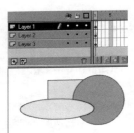

Figure 6.8 Reverse the layer order, and the stacking changes too.

For instance, if you were to have a Stage set up as shown in Figure 6.8, you could select the Paint Bucket tool and click on each of the shapes in turn – without having to select and deselect layers – in order to fill each shape with a new colour.

■ Guide layers

We've already identified that there are two types of guide layers:

1. Plain guide layers
2. Motion guide layers

We will return to motion guides in Chapter 8; to create a plain guide layer, however, you have to convert an existing layer into a plain guide layer. (You will remember that we can convert a layer in this way by going to the Layer Properties dialog box and clicking on the appropriate radio button.)

*You can also create a guide layer by right-clicking the layer you want to define as a guide and choosing **Guide** from the pop-up menu.*

There are many things you might wish to do with guide layers. For instance, you could place any objects on a guide layer to act as reference points when placing objects on other layers. These objects are not included in the final movie, however; they merely act as guides.

One particularly good use for guide layers is to place guidelines on them, similar to the guidelines used by page layout programs such as Quark Xpress. By using the **snap** feature (turned on from the **View** menu) you can then line up individual items to the guidelines in your guide layer.

It's a good idea to lock guide layers once you have set them up, so that you don't accidentally move the guides as you work with other layers.

■ Mask layers

A mask layer allows you to hide elements selectively in other layers that are linked to it – that is, elements in *masked* layers. You can think of a mask layer as an opaque sheet which has holes cut in it to allow you to see exactly what is underneath those holes, but no more.

Although it is possible to create an animated mask so that the window 'moves' over the masked layer, we'll stick for the moment with a static mask. (We'll cover animated masks in Chapter 8.)

Just as you cannot create a semi-transparent hole, the mask can only be applied or not applied. There is no such thing as a semi-transparent mask. What this means in practice is that anything you put down on your mask layer will allow whatever is on the masked layer to show through. Any areas of the mask layer left untouched will block out what is contained underneath on the masked layer.

To show this in practice, consider Figure 6.9. Here we have created two plain layers. A rectangle is drawn on Layer 1 and an oval on Layer 2. We have filled the oval with a gradient running from black to white.

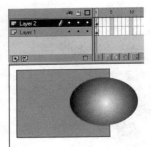

Figure 6.9 Two plain layers containing a rectangle and an oval respectively.

If we now convert Layer 2 into a mask layer (right-click on the name 'Layer 2' and select **mask**) and Layer 1 into its masked layer (in this case, as there are only two layers, Layer 1 automatically becomes the masked layer) you will see in Figure 6.10 that the area of the rectangle overlapped by the oval is visible, whilst the remainder of the rectangle is hidden.

Notice, too, that the amount of shading within the oval makes no difference to the amount of rectangle that is visible.

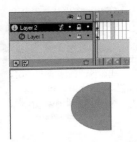

Figure 6.10 Layer 2 is now a mask layer with Layer 1 its masked layer.

If you want to make more than one masked layer attributable to one mask layer, you have to go to the Layer Properties dialog box (**Modify:Layer**) and then click on the radio button marked *Masked*, having first positioned the layer immediately below the mask layer.

In Figure 6.11 you can see that the mask layer is shown with a downward pointing arrow as its icon, whilst the masked layers each have a bent-arrow icon and are indented below the mask layer.

Figure 6.11 Each of the masked layers is indented and has a bent-arrow icon.

 A quick and easy way to create extra masked layers is to drag existing layers directly underneath the mask layer, or to select one of the masked layers and create a new layer by clicking on the + icon in the bottom left-hand corner of the Timeline.

When you create a mask layer with its masked sublayer you may not see anything different at first. This is because **for the masking to work you have to lock the mask layer and** *all* **masked layers beneath before masking takes effect.**

For example, in Figure 6.11 two of the masked layers shown, as well as the mask layer itself, do not have the padlock symbols shown against them. Only when all four layers have padlocks shown (i.e. are locked) will the complete masking show up on your Stage.

■ Paste in place

We saw in the last chapter how Flash allows you to paste objects from the Clipboard that have either been copied or cut from elsewhere within the Flash environment, or have been imported from another program.

Sometimes it is useful to copy or cut objects from different layers and paste them into one layer. Obviously it would be important to ensure that these objects are positioned exactly as they were in their original layers.

This is where **Paste in Place** comes in useful. If you copied (or cut) an object and simply pasted it into a new layer, Flash would always paste it in the centre of the Stage, ready for you to move and reposition.

However, if you go to the **Edit** menu and select **Paste in Place**, the exact positioning from the original layer will be replicated in this new layer.

*A shortcut for Paste in Place is to use the combination of **Ctrl-Shift-V**.*

7
Symbols and instances

■ Accessing libraries, symbols and instances

So far we've concentrated on the creation and manipulation of static objects. However, in a short while we will start to experiment with animations, and for that we will want to use copies of our objects over and over again as we place them in different parts of the scene, or use them in different movies.

Objects are stored in *libraries*, when they are then referred to as *symbols*. Each copy of the symbol used in your animation or movie is then referred to as an *instance*.

To access the library of the current movie that you are working on, go to your **Window** menu and select **Library**. You can also get there by keying **Ctrl-L** (Figure 7.1).

Figure 7.1 Access to the library of the current movie.

It is also possible to access symbols in libraries that you created for other movies. In this case you need to open up that particular library, which you do by going to the **File** menu and selecting **Open as Library** (or keying **Ctrl-Shift-O**) – see Figure 7.2.

Figure 7.2 Getting to the symbols in another movie library.

When you go to the library of another movie you will not be allowed to modify its contents. Only the current library can be modified, although you are allowed to copy symbols within another library to your current library.

Flash not only keeps a library with each and every movie you create, but it also has a collection of libraries which it stores with its program files. When you installed Flash you will have created five libraries that you can access via the **Libraries** menu (Figure 7.3). They are:

- buttons
- advanced buttons
- graphics
- movie clips
- sounds

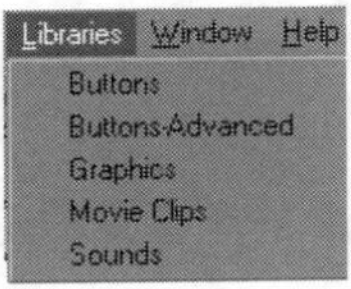

Figure 7.3 Five libraries of symbols are loaded by default with Flash 4.

If you were to go to your *program files* directory and look inside Flash 4 you would see a directory named *Libraries*. It contains matching files of the default libraries and each is a Flash file in its own right. If you wanted to add default libraries to this menu you therefore only have to copy your Flash .fla files to the directory (Figure 7.4).

Libraries

- Buttons.fla
- Buttons-Advanced.fla
- Graphics.fla
- Movie Clips.fla
- Sounds.fla

Figure 7.4 The Libraries directory within Flash's program files contains default library information.

You might find it worthwhile creating a special collection of symbols that you use repeatedly in your projects by copying them from existing movies into a special file just for this purpose.

When you open up a library you can view its contents in different ways and organise its contents the way you want to – with hierarchical folders, for instance.

Flash offers information on when the symbol was last modified, how many times it has been used and what type of item it is (Figure 7.5) You can expand and contract the window by clicking on the two respective icons at the top of the right-hand side slider bar. In expanded mode you can view the date that the symbol was last modified, and also count how many times it has been used. In the contracted mode you just get to see a list of the symbols in the library.

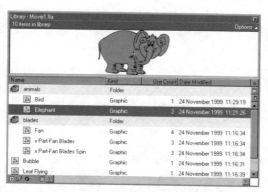

Figure 7.5 A view of the current library in expanded mode.

*By default, the Use Counter does not automatically update, as it might slow down the program. However, if you go to the **Options** button (shown in the top right-hand corner of figure 7.5) you can elect either to keep the Use Counts automatically updated, or to have it updated on demand (see Figure 7.6).*

Figure 7.6 From the Library Options menu you can update Use Counts when you want to.

You will also see in Figure 7.6 that the Options menu enables you to create new folders within a particular library. In Figure 7.5, for instance, there is a folder called *animals* which contains two symbols – *bird* and *elephant*. To add symbols to a particular folder, all you need do is drag the symbol on to the folder icon to create a hierarchy, which will prove to be especially useful when you have a library with many symbols in it.

You can also see at the bottom of Figure 7.5 that there are four icons in the bottom left-hand corner. These are, respectively:

1. New symbol
2. New folder
3. Symbol Properties
4. Delete item

We'll return to items 1 and 3 in a moment. Item 2 – Create new folder – is essentially the same as the *New Folder* option shown in Figure 7.6. Item 4 – Delete item – (also accessible from the Options menu) allows you to delete a selected library item, although a confirmation box first appears to check that you really do wish to delete the symbol, since this action cannot be reversed. **Remember that if you delete a symbol from your library, it will also be deleted from your movie; so if you are at all in doubt, check the *Use Count* before you delete any symbols.**

You can expand or close each library folder by double-clicking on it. This allows you more screen space to view the contents of other library folders.

▪ Creating symbols from graphic objects

There will be occasions when you will wish to re-use a graphic object that you have either made or imported into Flash. By converting the graphic into an object you will best be able to re-use it without affecting the original in any way.

With the static object selected on your stage go to the **Insert** menu and select **Convert to Symbol**. (You can instead press **F8**.) The Symbol Properties dialog box will appear (Figure 7.7) which allows you to choose whether you are creating a symbol of a graphic, a button or a movie clip. It also gives it a default name based on the number of symbols already in the library, but it is usually best if you give it a name that is meaningful so that you can locate the symbol easily at a later time.

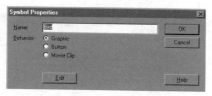

Figure 7.7 The Symbol Properties dialog box.

Once you have clicked **OK** the object on the Stage becomes an *instance* of the new symbol you have created.

 You are no longer able to edit the graphic object directly on your Stage once you have converted it into a symbol. Instead you have to enter symbol editing mode (see below) to do so.

■ Creating new symbols without conversion

If you wish to create a symbol that is to be used many times, it is not necessary to create a graphic first and then convert it to a symbol. Instead, you can create a symbol from scratch directly in **Symbol Editing** mode. Click on **New Symbol** in either the menu (Figure 7.6) or on its icon (Figure 7.5) to produce a new blank symbol.

Figure 7.8 Enter Symbol Editing mode via the click button at the top–right hand corner of the Stage.

The Symbol Editing entry button can be found at the top right-hand corner of the stage (see Figure 7.8) and this will bring up a drop-down list of available symbols, including your new blank symbol, which you can now select for editing.

You'll know you're in Symbol Editing mode rather than working on the Stage because in the top left corner of the Stage area is another pair of buttons, similar to those in Figure 7.9, which show the current editing status.

Figure 7.9 You can return to the normal Stage editing mode by clicking on the left button tag.

If you have more than one scene in your movie, you can select which scene to edit by selecting the scene button tag just as you would when switching back from Symbol Editing to Stage Editing as shown in Figure 7.9.

■ Symbols vs objects

At this stage you might well be wondering why one should go to all the bother of using symbols when it is possible to re-use objects simply by copying them to another part of the stage.

Well, of course you can work in that way if you want to; but by converting objects to symbols Flash only has to store the set of vector instructions for that object once. By then using multiple instances of that one symbol, Flash does not need to redefine the vector parameters each time the symbol is used. Instead it looks up its library of symbols and gleans the information from there.

Flash could then modify the different instances of each symbol – say, rotating it, colouring it, or whatever. But the basic set of instructions remains unaltered, and it is this that allows Flash to save a great deal of information in a compact file.

To place an instance of a symbol on to your stage:

1. Select the layer on which you wish to place the instance.
2. Open the library containing the symbol whose instance you want to import.
3. Click once on the symbol to preview it in the upper library window (Figure 7.5).
4. Drag the preview to the Stage where you want to place your instance.
5. Release the mouse.

You could, if you wished, skip the preview stage and simply drag the symbol name to the Stage.

■ Changing an instance in an instant

We just mentioned that it is possible to change the appearance of an instance without altering the original symbol. In particular we can:

1. Scale it
2. Rotate it
3. Change its colour
4. Change its transparency

Scaling and rotation is carried out in exactly the same way as you would scale or rotate any other object (see page 37); but you alter the colour and transparency by calling up the Instance Properties dialog box. Double-click on the instance to open the dialog box and then click on the **Color Effect** tab. Immediately you are offered a choice of the following:

■ brightness
■ tint
■ alpha
■ special

If we decided to alter the brightness of one of a pair of instances, for instance, we would double-click on the relevant instance on the Stage, then select the **Color Effect** tab and select **Brightness** (Figure 7.10). The amount of brightness can be altered either by tweaking the slider tab or by entering an amount directly into the brightness value box.

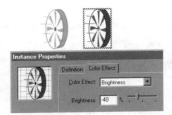

Figure 7.10 Altering different instances of the same symbol.

Similarly, we can change the colour balance by selecting **Tint**
from the **Color Effect** options. Here we can not only choose the
colour we want – either by keying in values to the RGB boxes,
or by clicking on the colour grid – but also set the degree of tint-
ing to be applied to the instance, again by using either the slider
control or by entering an exact amount into the **Color Effect** box
(Figure 7.11).

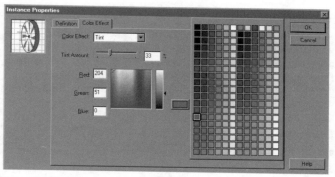

Figure 7.11 Changing an instance's colour settings.

If we want to alter the transparency of the instance we change its
Alpha setting. A 100% setting makes it completely opaque; a 0%
setting sets it transparent. Once again we can use either the slider or enter a number directly into the Alpha box (Figure 7.12).

Figure 7.12 Setting the Alpha channel to 100% makes the instance totally opaque.

Flash 4 also allows you to simultaneously change a symbol
instance's colour and transparency. For this, you need to select
Special from the **Color Effect** options. In Figure 7.13 you can see

that all of the colour and alpha channels have two sliders. This may at first cause some confusion. Basically the left and right sliders have different jobs to do. The *left* sliders cause changes in the values of the original colour balance whilst the *right* sliders add colour to the entire object.

Figure 7.13 The special settings allow you to alter transparency along with the colour balance.

Imagine, for instance, that you have three circles within your instance. One is coloured pure red (i.e. it has an RGB value of 255,0,0); another is pure green whilst the third is pure blue.

If you move the left-hand blue slider to the left, it will reduce the amount of blue in the blue circle, but will have no effect on the green or red circles since they have no blue element within them. However, if you slide the right-hand blue slider to the right, it adds blue to everything, including both the red and green circles, and these will now start to change colour.

As is usual, a little experimentation will soon make this clear.

 *Sometimes you might want to swap over one instance for another **after** you have made changes to its size, rotation, colour, or whatever. Flash 4 makes this easy. Having made any modifications to the original instance, double-click on it to open up its Properties dialog box. This time, you need to click on the **Definition** tab (see Figure 7.14) where you will see your current instance highlighted with a bullet point. Select an alternative symbol from the list on offer. The bullet will remain with the original symbol. Now click on the **Switch Symbol** button to swap the old for the new, while keeping all your modifications in place.*

Figure 7.14 Using the Switch option in the Definition section of the Properties dialog box.

If, instead of swapping one instance with another, you wish to edit a symbol, you can use the **Edit Symbol** button to the right of the Switch Symbol button we just mentioned. Remember, though, that when you edit a symbol, rather than an instance, it will not only change the symbol that resides in your library, but also every instance of the symbol within your movie.

■ Breaking the link between instance and symbol

Finally, there may be occasions when you want to break the link between an instance of a particular symbol and the symbol itself. For example, you might wish to change the shape of a symbol in certain places, but not in others.

The best way to do this is to select the instance of the symbol whose link you want to break. Then from the **Modify** menu select **Break Apart** (or **Ctrl-B**).

You can then alter the shape (or other parameter) of this object and even save it once more as a new symbol if you are likely to need this new shape again.

8 Animation

■ Animation basics

For obvious reasons, we have so far taken up almost half this
book looking at the basics of using Flash. However, it is only
when we move on to the use of animations that Flash really
comes into its own. It is, after all, probably the main reason that
you bought the software in the first place.

In Flash you can:

- move an object across the Stage;
- increase or decrease its size;
- rotate the object;
- change its colour;
- change its basic shape; and
- make it fade in or fade out.

There are two basic methods one can use in creating a Flash
animation:

1. Make frames individually.
2. Create starting and ending frames and let Flash 'tween'
   between them.

■ Frame types

If you look at the Timeline you will see that there are many cells,
or **protoframes** which define individual frames within your
movie. Assuming you have a totally blank Flash Stage, you will
see that the first protoframe contains a hollow bullet. This type
of bullet signifies that there are, at present, no images contained
within this frame. Later, when we place an object into a frame,
the bullet will turn solid (see Figure 8.1).

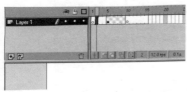

Figure 8.1 The hollow bullet in Keyframe 1 shows that it contains nothing. Clicking on frame 2 will continue to display a blank Stage.

Whenever you place an object within the Timeline of a movie, you have to create a **keyframe**. Normally you would leave some of the protoframes blank between the first keyframe and the next keyframe – we'll see why in a moment.

If, say, you place an object in the first keyframe and a second object in your second keyframe, the frames in between the two keyframes would continue to show whatever had been placed in the first keyframe (see Figures 8.2 and 8.3).

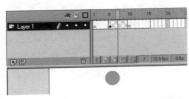

Figure 8.2 We have placed a filled circle in Frame 5 (note the solid bullet) so clicking on Frame 7 will continue to show the circle.

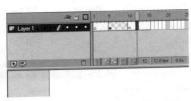

Figure 8.3 In Frame 10 we have removed the circle; hence Frame 12 displays nothing.

*You can alter the size with which you view the Timeline in order to see more or fewer frames. Go to the **Frame View** pop-up menu to the top right of the Stage and select an option (see Figure 8.4).*

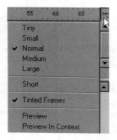

Figure 8.4 Select your Timeline size from the Frame View pop-up menu.

To add keyframes to your Timeline you can either go to the **Insert** menu or right-click on the particular protoframe you wish to make into a keyframe. The latter is much quicker and easier!

Whichever way you choose, you will notice that you have the option to either:

1. Insert Blank Keyframe
2. Insert Keyframe

If you wish to change the contents of the scene completely at this point, then go for option 1. If you intend to make minor changes, then plump for option 2. The latter duplicates whatever has gone before, allowing you to add objects, move things around, or whatever.

If you look once again at Figure 8.3, you will notice that there are vertical black lines before Frames 5 and 10 in the timeline showing, in effect, where the contents of each keyframe run out. There is also grey shading between Frames 5 and 10 showing that there is content in these particular frames.

*Although Flash talks about 'inserting' keyframes, it actually does nothing of the sort! What it really does is to convert an existing protoframe into a keyframe. The number of frames remains constant. If instead you use the **Insert Frame** command, then Flash does add extra frames.*

You may quite often find the need to insert extra frames – and a quick way to do this, apart from laboriously inserting single frames, is to copy and paste empty frames from the end of the Timeline into the point in the Timeline you wish to expand. However, you cannot simply copy and paste using the normal Windows shortcuts, otherwise you will paste over whatever frames are already in existence. Instead, right-click on your selected number of empty frames and select **Copy Frames** or **Paste Frames** as appropriate.

*You can also copy and paste frames by using the keyboard with **Ctrl-Alt-C** or **Ctrl-Alt-V** as appropriate.*

Just as there are two commands for inserting frames – depending on whether you wish to add an extra frame, rather than a keyframe – so, too, are there two commands (confusingly contained in the **Insert** menu!) for removing frames:

1. Clear Keyframe
2. Delete Frame

The former simply removes the keyframe status from your selected frame. It does not remove it from the Timeline. The latter, on the other hand, deletes the frame entirely from your movie and reduces the number of frames accordingly.

Sometimes when you try to delete a keyframe it appears that Flash refuses to carry out your instructions. This is most likely to happen if you try to delete a keyframe without deleting the contents of the in-between frames that have picked up their information from the keyframe you are trying to delete. In its attempt to make sense of your conflicting instructions, Flash creates a virtual keyframe. The result is that you end up trying to delete a keyframe which Flash replaces with an identical one! Instead, select all the associated in-between frames with your keyframe and delete the lot in one go.

■ Making a simple animation

Let's kick off by creating an extremely simple animation using frame-by-frame animation. Open up a new Flash document and switch on the grid (**View:Grid**) for ease of accurate placing. Select the first frame and on your Stage draw a circle.

Next, click on the second frame and insert a keyframe as described above. Straight away two things happen: a bullet is added to show that Frame 2 is now a keyframe, and the circle you drew before becomes selected. Drag the selected circle to a new position a few centimetres to the right. Repeat once more with the third frame (see Figure 8.5).

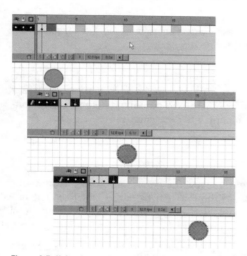

Figure 8.5 Using Insert Keyframe commands to duplicate and move the circle.

If you now click Frames 1, 2 and 3 in turn you will see the circle 'move' to its new positions. However, to see your movie automatically, go to your **Control** menu and select **Play**. It's all over pretty quickly, but if instead you go to **Control:Loop Playback** and then **Play** the scene again it will continue looping through your movie.

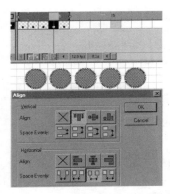

Figure 8.8 By using the Edit Multiple Frames option you can align and space each of the object instances.

Setting the frame rate

Flash allows you to set the frame rate which determines how many frames are displayed per second. Set the frame rate too fast, and the movie will rush past in a blur. Too slow, and the animation will be jerky. Normally, the standard rate for a feature film is 25 frames per second (fps). On the Web, 12 fps is a good rate. By default, Flash sets the frame rate at 12 fps.

To change the default setting, which affects the entire movie, go to the **Modify** menu and select **Movie**. Alternatively you can double-click the Frame Rate value at the bottom of the Timeline. The **Movie Properties** dialog box appears (Figure 8.9).

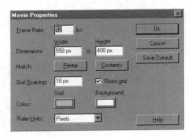

Figure 8.9 Setting the frame rate in the Movie Properties dialog box.

Although the frame rate of a movie remains constant, you can speed up or slow down a particular section of a movie by adding or deleting frames from that section. Inserting in-between frames adds very little to the overall file size, but if you add extra keyframes in order to show the object in a slightly different position each time, the overall movie file will increase in size.

 *We saw in Figure 8.4 that it is possible to increase the size of the frame representations within the Timeline. From that same drop-down menu you can select either **Preview** or **Preview in Context** which will give you previews of your individual frames either at full size or in relation to one another. See Figure 8.10 to see the difference.*

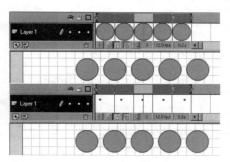

Figure 8.10 Preview (top) and Preview in Context (bottom).

■ Tweening animation

Frame-by-frame animation has two major drawbacks associated with it. It is extremely time-consuming, and it also creates very large files. By using **Tweening** Flash gets round both of these problems.

 The word 'tweening' is derived from the action of creating in-between frames, which is what cartoon animators used to do laboriously by hand when creating cartoon feature films.

Tweening comes in two forms:

1. motion tweening
2. shape tweening

By defining the beginning and end keyframes, Flash creates a series of frames with incremental changes that change the first Keyframe to the last keyframe, morphing from one to the other.

Let's create a simple motion tween to move a circle from the left of our Stage to the right. Firstly create a new movie and, in Keyframe 1, add a circle to the Stage, just as we did before in the previous exercise (see Figure 8.11).

With Frame 1 still selected, select **Create Motion Tween** from the **Insert** menu. The circle is made into a symbol which Flash calls, by default, 'Tween 1'. Now select Frame 10 and **Insert:Frame**. A dotted line appears in the Timeline showing there is an unresolved tween operation.

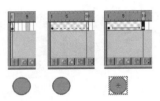

Figure 8.11 Creating a motion tween.

Convert Frame 10 to a keyframe, however, and the tween information thinks it is complete. The dotted line turns into an arrow. However, so far nothing has changed. Select the circle in Frame 10 and move it to a new position and now, when you **Play** the animation (or press **Enter**) the circle moves smoothly from one side to the other.

You can view the tweening that has been created by looking at the individual frames with Onion Skinning turned on (Figure 8.12).

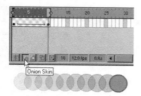

Figure 8.12 Viewing the motion tween with Onion Skins showing.

You can add extra keyframes into an already-created motion tween, allowing you to alter the path of the animation if you want to.

If you look at Figure 8.12 you will see that an arrow links Frame 0 to Frame 10. Using the right-click menu, insert a keyframe on Frame 6. The circle appropriate to the tween position at Frame 6 is highlighted. Now, drag the circle instance to a new position and let go (Figure 8.13).

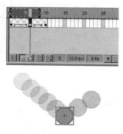

Figure 8.13 Inserting an extra keyframe into a motion tween.

Now when you play your animation, the redefined path will be substituted for your original path.

Tweening colour changes and fading in and out

As well as using Motion Tween to move objects around the Stage, you can also use it to change the colours of objects, or even to fade an object in and out of the picture.

Let's start once again with a circle positioned in Frame 1.

Figure 8.14 Start with a circle in Frame 1.

You can motion tween grouped objects or symbols, so we first convert this circle into a symbol by clicking on **Insert:Convert to Symbol**. In the Timeline we next create a new keyframe at, say, Frame 10. With keyframe 10 still selected, go to the Modify menu and select **Instance**. With the dialog box that appears, you will see the second tab is labelled **Color Effect**. By choosing this and then selecting **Tint** in the drop-down menu we can select a new colour for our circle (Figure 8.15).

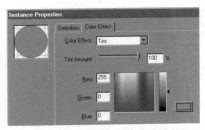

Figure 8.15 Changing the colour of the instance.

If, instead of changing colour, you wish to fade out the object, choose **Alpha** from the drop-down menu (Figure 8.16). The Alpha setting determines the transparency of your object. A zero-value effectively washes your object completely from the picture.

Finally you can test your colour change by playing your animation in the normal way.

Figure 8.16 Changing the transparency of the instance with its Alpha channel.

Tweening objects that change size

Not only can you create a motion tween that moves your object and changes colour, but you can also change its size (Figure 8.17). In your final keyframe resize the instance, but before you try out your animation, double-click on one of the frames to open up the Frame Properties dialog box. Ensure that the tick box labelled **Tween Scaling** is selected.

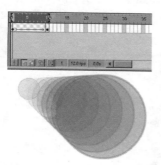

Figure 8.17 Onion skins show a motion tween for an object that changes size as it moves.

Rotating objects

If you want to rotate an object as part of your motion tween, you need to give more information than two keyframes can offer. If you think about it, an object could rotate clockwise or anticlockwise, or even flip over. Flash allows you to define the method of rotation by bringing up the Frame Properties dialog box when you double-click on one of the tweening frames (Figure 8.18).

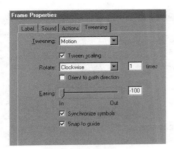

Figure 8.18 Determining the direction of rotation.

You can also slow down the rotation at the start or end of the spin by sliding the **Easing** slider to the right or left, depending on whether you want to 'ease in' or 'ease out'.

Moving objects along a pre-defined path

It's all very well to be able to move objects around the Stage in a collection of straight lines, but in real life you will want to move the objects along curves and trajectories as well. This is where motion guides come into their own.

Motion guides define the paths for a tweened object to move along. Each guide has to be created on a separate layer, but you can use one guide to control a number of objects on different layers.

To create a motion guide layer start off a new Flash document and place an object in the first frame. Convert it into a symbol (**Insert:Convert to Symbol**) and then create a straight line tween to, say, Frame 20 as explained above (see Figure 8.19).

At the bottom of the Timeline we next click the **Add Guide Layer** button (Figure 8.20) which adds a new layer directly above the layer you selected. The layer you were working on is now indented under the guide layer.

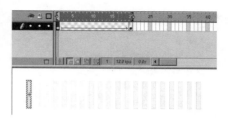

Figure 8.19 Start by creating a straight line tween.

Figure 8.20 Adding a guide layer creates a new layer above your active layer.

Once you have selected this guide layer you can now draw the path you want your object to follow by using the Pencil, Oval, Rectangle, Line or Brush tools. In the Frame Properties dialog box ensure the **Snap to guide** check box is ticked (see Figure 8.18) and then tweak the start and end objects directly over the ends of the motion path you have just defined. Although the motion path is visible at present (Figure 8.21), it will not be shown in the final movie.

 It's a good idea, once you have created your motion path, to lock this layer so that you cannot alter it accidentally.

In Figure 8.21 you can see that the object – although it slavishly follows the motion path – remains at its original angle. In normal motion you would expect the object to twist and turn in sympathy with the direction of movement.

This time, therefore, ensure that the **Orient to path direction** check box shown in Figure 8.18 is checked. The object should now always face the direction of movement (Figure 8.22).

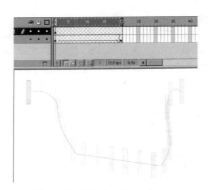

Figure 8.21 The object follows the defined motion path.

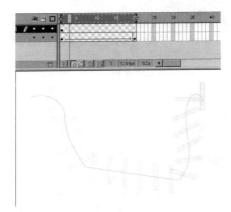

Figure 8.22 The object now rotates in the direction of movement.

 If you have sudden changes of direction in your motion guide, Flash may have difficulty in aligning the object at every frame. If your moving object looks as if it needs a bit of help, there is nothing to stop you inserting an extra keyframe or two and manually realigning the direction each instance faces.

Shape tweening

Just as you can tween objects to make them move from one part of the stage to another, so too can you get an object to morph into another. This type of tweening is called **shape tweening**.

Just as in motion tweening, shape tweening requires you to define the beginning and end shape; Flash then creates the in-between frames morphing one shape gradually into the next.

 It may seem obvious when you think of it, but it is important to understand that whereas motion tweening works on groups and symbols, shape tweening requires the objects to be editable in order to work (Figure 8.23).

> ⚠ Shape tweening will not occur on layers containing symbols or grouped objects.

Figure 8.23 Flash warns you if you try to shape tween the wrong type of object.

There are some functions that shape tweening can do that can also be carried out in motion tweening. The shape that you wish to tween to might, for instance, be a different colour from your original shape. It follows, therefore, that shape tweening can be instructed to change an object's colour as well as its size and location. You cannot, however, get Flash to rotate an object or move it along a motion guide using shape tweening.

Let's start by transforming a circle into a square – an example of morphing simple lines and fills. We'll create a new Flash document and draw a circle in Frame 1 (Figure 8.24). For ease of demonstration we will make the circle in outline form only, although we could just as easily have made it filled.

Next we select Frame 10 in the Timeline, but this time we'll **Insert** a **Blank Keyframe** which has the effect of removing everything from the Stage at this particular frame. Now we can create a square on the Stage (Figure 8.25). Don't worry about the exact placing of the square right now. We can worry about that later.

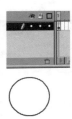

Figure 8.24 A circle is placed in Frame 1.

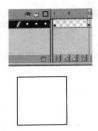

Figure 8.25 A square is placed in Frame 10.

Next, we open up the Frame Properties dialog box by double-clicking, or right-clicking, on one of the in-between frames (2 to 9) and selecting the **Tweening** tab. In the drop-down menu we select **Shape Tweening** (Figure 8.26). The **Blend Type** radio buttons allow you to choose whether you want Flash to retain any sharp corners and straight lines as it transforms from one shape to another (**Angular**) or if you want it to smooth out the tweening shapes (**Distributive**). As before, the **Easing** slider allows you to change the transition speed at either the start or end of the tween.

When we click **OK**, Flash morphs the circle into a square. On the Timeline, if we have Tinted Frames active (which is set in the pop-up menu at the end of the Timeline – see Figure 8.4) then Flash turns the frames containing the shape tween light green.

■■

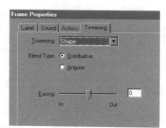

Figure 8.26 Selecting Shape Tweening in the Frame Properties dialog box.

We can see the individual stages of the morph if we turn on onion skinning (Figure 8.27).

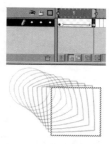

Figure 8.27 Onion skinning allows us to view the entire morph.

The onion skinning shows clearly that the circle and square are not nearly aligned. By choosing either Frame 1 or Frame 10 we can nudge the circle or square one on top of the other so that they are perfectly aligned (Figure 8.28).

Shape tweening multiple objects

Because Flash would have difficulty in determining which starting shape morphs to which ending shape if you had more than one object on a particular layer, it is advisable to restrict yourself to a single object on any layer you wish to shape tween.

Figure 8.28 At last the circle and square are perfectly aligned.

This is best illustrated if we attempt to create the following morph. We'll place a square and circle on one layer and ask Flash to morph to the same square and circle, but placed in a different area of the Stage. As you can see from Figure 8.29, Flash has chosen to morph the square into the circle and vice versa in preference to crossing their morphing paths.

Figure 8.29 The circle and square have morphed into one another in preference to crossing over.

Using Shape Hints to improve your morphing

When we transformed a circle into a square it was fairly obvious how Flash would morph the shape. Sometimes, however, especially with complicated shapes, Flash has difficulty in interpreting exactly what you want it to do. You can help it by providing **Shape Hints**.

Say that you wanted to morph the bird in Figure 8.30 into an elephant. (We've actually used two images in Flash's library of symbols. As you cannot shape tween symbols or grouped objects we had to break them apart first using the **Modify** menu.)

Figure 8.30 Preparing to morph a bird into an elephant.

We begin by placing the bird in Frame 1 and inserting a blank keyframe in Frame 10 where the elephant is then placed. Bring up the Frame Properties dialog box and ask it to shape tween from one animal to the other.

Select Frame 1 if it is not already selected and either go to your **Modify** menu and choose **Transform:Add Shape Hint** or – far quicker – key **Ctrl-H**. A little red spot appears in the centre of the bird image which is exactly duplicated in the centre of the elephant image when you move across to Frame 10. This red spot marks your first shape hint's position. Unlike the way in which some morphing programs work, it is important in Flash to place shape hints in order (either clockwise or anticlockwise) around the *edge* of the object. So drag the red spot, say, to the top of the bird's head and then, in Frame 10, drag the red spot to the top of the elephant's head.

Straight away the elephant's shape hint turns green, whilst the bird's shape hint turns yellow. Continue to place shape hints around the edge of each animal (Figure 8.31) so that Flash is given help in determining which parts of the bird morph to their respective elephant parts.

Figure 8.31 Seven shape hints have been added to help with the morph.

If you think you have made a mistake with the placing of your shape hints, you can reposition them at any time you want. Alternatively, you can remove a shape hint by clicking on the initial keyframe and then dragging the hint off the Stage.

Getting shape tweens to move along a path

We've already said that you cannot use shape tweening to move an object along a guide path. So what do you do if you want a circle, say, to turn into a square, but to move along a loop as it does so? The answer is to use a combination of shape tweening and motion tweening.

As we did before, create a shape tween to morph a circle into a square. Let's do it over 20 frames, so that the last keyframe is defined as Frame 20. Now select all 20 frames in the tween sequence and, using the **Insert** menu, convert all 20 frames to keyframes.

Flash keeps the tween information within each keyframe that you have just created. As Flash allows you to place any keyframe object where you want to, it is a simple matter to drag each instance to a position on the stage. For more accuracy, you could create a new guide layer and draw a curved line on it. Go to the **View** menu and select **Snap**. Now when you drag the object close to the guide line it should snap into place against the line.

■ Reversing frames

Sometimes a seemingly complex animation can be made much simpler by reversing a sequence of some of your frames. For instance, if an object grows and then shrinks, then why not save yourself time and effort by creating the growth sector and then simply copying and reversing these frames for the second part of the animation.

Flash can do this very easily. In your Timeline, select the frames you want to copy by highlighting them and then selecting **Copy Frames** from the Frame Properties dialog box (Figure 8.32).

Figure 8.32 Copying frames using the Frame Properties dialog box.

Now paste these frames into position immediately behind the frames you have created using the same menu. Your animation now contains two growth animations, one immediately following the other. Select the second set of frames that you have just pasted and, from your **Modify** menu, select **Frames:Reverse**. Flash reverses the order of the second set of frames creating the illusion of an object growing and then contracting.

■ Animated masks

We learned in Chapter 6 that you can selectively hide or reveal objects by using mask layers. There is no reason why that mask should not, itself, be a moving object. You can use any of the three types of tweening – motion tweening, shape tweening or frame-by-frame animation – to create a moving mask.

If we wanted some text to be revealed by a 'spotlight' over time, we could make a mask that contained a solid circle which was motion tweened across the Stage. Any text in the associated masked layer would then automatically be revealed as the circle moved over it.

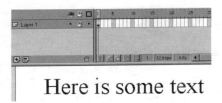

Figure 8.33 First we add some text to the Stage.

The first thing, then, is to add some text somewhere on the Stage (Figure 8.33) and then to create, say, 10 keyframes along its Timeline. Remember, each keyframe will contain the whole of our text message. Now create a mask layer and in Frame 1 of this mask layer place a solid circle over the start of the text (Figure 8.34). Remember that you will need to unlock the mask layer in order to be able to edit it!

Figure 8.34 Keyframes are added, and then a mask layer with circle.

Next we create a motion tween along the mask layer such that the circle ends up at the right-hand end of the text at the end of the tween process (Figure 8.35).

Figure 8.35 Motion tweening is added to the mask layer.

If we turn on our onion skin view we can see that a series of circles runs along the text (Figure 8.36). Remember that any solid area in the mask layer allows us to see the layer below; any clear area in the mask hides the area below. The effect, when you run **Control:Test Movie**, is text that is sequentially highlighted by a moving circle. Very impressive output for very little work!

Figure 8.36 Onion skin view gives a good indication of the mask path.

■ Saving your animations

So, we've created our tweened image and we could, if we wanted, simply save it along with the rest of the movie. However, we've already seen that if it is at all possible that the same sequence could be reused, it will take up much less memory if we save this moving sequence as a graphic symbol in its own right and then re-use the graphic symbol from our library.

Flash allows us to save moving images in one of two ways:

1. animated graphic symbol
2. movie clip symbol

Animated symbols are unable to save any sound tracks or inter-active features (both of which we'll be covering later). Movie clips, on the other hand, are self-contained and can be saved in just one frame of your movie frames. If you are likely to want to edit an instance of your animation when it is re-used, you should save it as an animated symbol.

To create an animated graphic symbol, highlight all the frames in all the layers you want to save and **Edit:Copy frames**. Next, create a new symbol by selecting **Insert:New Symbol**. From the resulting Properties dialog box choose **Graphic**.

Once you click on **OK** a new symbol is created in the library, but it has just one frame and one Timeline. In Frame 1 Selecting **Edit:Paste Frames** to copy the animation frames into their own new symbol.

*The only clue that a library symbol is actually an animated symbol is by looking in the top right-hand corner of the library window. An animated symbol has **Stop** and **Play** buttons showing with which you can preview your animation.*

Remember when you come to use the animated symbol later on to allow enough frames to contain the entire symbol clip; unless, of course, you want to have overlapping Timelines to allow simultaneous actions.

To create a movie clip symbol, you do exactly the same as before when saving an animated symbol, except that you choose **Movie Clip** rather than **Graphic** in the Symbol Properties dialog box.

Movie clips have their own Timeline and will play continuously until such time as a new blank keyframe is placed within that Timeline to stop the movie running. Unlike animated graphic symbols, movie clips need to be exported to a test mode before they can be viewed. This is simple enough, however. From your

Control menu choose either **Test Movie** or **Test Scene** to get Flash to export the movie clip to a shockwave format (.swf) file which it will then display.

■ A note about scenes

Creating a movie with 10 or 20 frames is easy enough to handle; but what happens if your final movie runs to hundreds of frames? You could, in theory, scroll backwards and forwards along the Timeline finding the relevant bits of your movie. It's much easier, however, to break the movie up into manageable sized chunks called *scenes*.

You can create scenes and arrange the order in which they play by going to **Window:Inspector:Scene** (Figure 8.37).

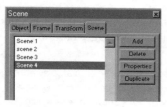

Figure 8.37 The Scene Inspector window.

Each scene title can be dragged one above the other to change the order in which they play. Once Flash has finished with one scene it automatically starts playing the next one.

It follows, therefore, that in order to maintain continuity between scenes it is a good idea to copy the entire contents of each layer of the last frame of your current scene to the beginning frame of the next scene in order to ensure the accurate placing of any elements on the Stage.

You can tell at a glance which scene you are currently editing by the flag that comes up to the left of the Timeline – as in Figure 8.38.

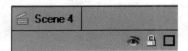

Figure 8.38 Flash leaves you in no doubt which scene you are currently editing.

Scenes are particularly useful when using interactivity within your movie: 'If such an event happens then jump to scene 5; otherwise jump to scene 7' for instance.

We will be examining interactive movies in the next chapter. See you there!

9 Interactivity

So far we've been concentrating on sequential animation – where Flash moves from one scene to the next, for instance. However, there is no reason why you cannot instruct Flash to move from the end of one sequence to the start of another, or from any point in a scene to any other scene or frame you wish.

You give instructions to Flash by assigning actions to frames and buttons. A frame with an action assigned to it has an 'a' displayed within the Timeline (see Figure 9.1).

Figure 9.1 An 'a' is displayed in keyframes containing actions.

You'll save yourself time and eye strain if you assign action frames to one layer of your Timeline only. That way, when you are searching for an action frame in the middle of a long movie it will be much easier to find. Name the layer 'Actions' and lock it so that you cannot assign objects to it by accident.

▪ Action types

There are two types of action in Flash:

1. frame actions
2. button actions

The first refers to actions that need no user input to generate the action. When the movie reaches a particular action frame in its playback it carries out the instruction. Individual frames can each contain many actions. A button action, on the other hand, requires input from the user before it carries out the instruction.

Frame actions

An action is assigned to a frame from the Frame Properties dialog box, accessed as usual by right-clicking on the frame and selecting **Properties** (Figure 9.2).

Figure 9.2 Actions are added from the Frame Properties dialog box.

With the Actions tab selected, you can bring up a menu of available commands by clicking on the + button (Figure 9.3).

Figure 9.3 Bringing up the Actions menu.

We'll look at these actions in more detail later on. But clicking on any one of these action options will then bring up a parameters box to the right of the listed action (Figure 9.4).

Figure 9.4 The parameters for the action appear to the right of the listed action.

You can keep on adding actions to this one frame so that, for example, you turn on anti-aliasing to improve the quality of the playback, you stop all sounds which might still be playing from previous instructions and you pause the movie until another instruction tells it to resume. This sequence is shown in Figure 9.5. You can, of course, also remove previously inserted actions by highlighting the particular action and then clicking on the – button.

Figure 9.5 Multiple actions can be assigned to one frame.

Note on the right-hand side of the actions list that there are up and down buttons. These let you alter the order in which the actions are carried out. Flash always starts from the top of the list and works its way downwards. So, for instance, if there were two instructions – one of which took you to another frame and the second of which took you to a new URL (Uniform Resource Locator or, more simply, Web page address), then if the former was at the top of the list you would always be taken to the new frame, whilst if the latter headed up the action list you would always be redirected to the new URL.

You can easily check what actions are associated with a particular action frame by hovering your mouse cursor over the frame. In the scenario above, for example, you would get a message as shown in Figure 9.6 – assuming, that is, that you have **Tooltips** turned on in your preference choices (**File:Preferences**).

Figure 9.6 Tooltips gives you an indication of the actions you have programmed in.

■ Frame labels and comments

Although you can easily tell Flash to jump to a particular frame from one of your action frames, it is often better (especially in longer movies) to give your target frame a label and to instruct Flash to jump to the label rather than the frame number. If you were to insert or delete frames after specifying a frame number you might have to redefine your jumps, so the use of labels obviates this.

Sometimes, too, for frames that are not the targets of action frames, it is useful to add comments about the frame that describes what is happening. This often makes it easier at a later date to pick up from where you left off programming the movie.

Flash allows you to place either labels or comments on any frame, but you cannot add both to one frame. You add them by going to the Frame Properties dialog box and selecting the **Label** tab (Figure 9.7).

Figure 9.7 Add labels or comments from the Frame Properties dialog box.

When you add a label, the Timeline will add a little red flag to the frame and display as much of the label as it can. A comment will instead have the effect of adding two green slashes as well as the comment to the Timeline representation. Sometimes, however, there may not be room to see the entire comment or label because of a following keyframe, but you can always see the tooltip associated with the label or comment (Figure 9.8).

Figure 9.8 By having a layer for actions and another for comments, you can get the best of both worlds!

■ Some basic actions

We saw in Figure 9.3 that there are plenty of actions that you can associate with a particular frame. We'll consider just three of them for the moment, though.

The **Stop** and **Play** actions are two of the most fundamental. You add these to any frame to control the playback of the movie at particular points. You might want, for instance, a moving animation to begin and then pause until such time as another action is completed, and then resume once again. You can also override the playback defaults of the finished Shockwave format (.swf) file or projector file – both of which we'll be examining in Chapter 12 – to make them play or pause when first they start up.

When you add either of these actions, there are no additional parameters to enter (Figure 9.9).

Figure 9.9 Neither Stop nor Play actions need additional parameters.

Unlike the use of Stop and Play, the **Go To** action needs you to enter additional parameters for Flash to know what you want it to do. By default (Figure 9.4) Flash is told to stop when it gets to a new frame, the default scene is the current one and the target frame is the first one in the current frame.

It is easy to change the defaults. To make Flash resume playing once it has reached its new location, tick the check box that reads **Go to and Play** (which you can see at the bottom of Figure 9.4). From the drop-down list to the right of the scene window you can select which scene to go to and using the radio buttons below you can select which frame you wish to go to.

Say, for instance, that we wish our action frame to whisk us away to Frame 6 of Scene 5, then Figure 9.10 shows us what the action parameter box would look like:

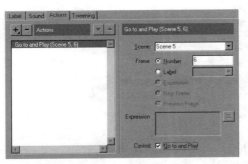

Figure 9.10 Flash is directed to jump to Frame 6 of Scene 5 from this action frame, and then to start playing straight away.

We'll look at some of the expression possibilities later on. You will notice how it is also easy to specify that Flash should jump to either the previous or next frame by clicking their appropriate radio buttons once the current scene is elected.

There is no reason why you could not specify the name of a frame or scene, even if it has not yet been defined – as long as you are organised enough to know in advance what your naming conventions are going to be!

To try out your specified actions, you can use the **Test Movie** or **Test Scene** options in the **Control** menu; if you try simply using **Enter** in editing mode the actions will, by default, be disabled. This is to stop you being whisked off to destinations unknown when you are trying to work on a specific part of the Timeline. You can, however, switch on the actions by going to your **Control** menu and clicking on **Enable Frame Actions** (Figure 9.11).

Figure 9.11 Enabling the editor to preview your actions.

■ Buttons

One of the most basic ways in which you can get your audience to participate in the running of your movie is to allow them to interact with the movie by using buttons.

Buttons are basically symbols that can display a different image for each of their possible states. A button can only ever have four frames associated with it and these are:

1. The **Up** state – which represents the button when the mouse cursor is not over the button.
2. The **Over** state – which occurs when the mouse cursor is hovering over the button.
3. The **Down** state – which shows what the button looks like when it is clicked.

4. The **Hit** state – which you never see within the final movie, but which defines an area over which the button will respond.

It is perfectly acceptable to include movie clips within different button frames to display animated buttons.

Creating a new button

Simple buttons are easily created using basic geometric shapes. If you change the characteristics of the shapes within the different button states then it will be easy for your audience to know that your shapes are actually buttons.

Start by creating a new symbol by going to your **Insert** menu and selecting **New Symbol** (Figure 9.12).

Figure 9.12 Insert a new symbol from the *Insert* menu.

In the resulting Symbol Properties dialog box you can specify a new name for your symbol if you like, but you must select **Button** behaviour (Figure 9.13).

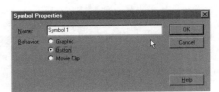

Figure 9.13 Set the symbol behaviour to *Button*.

A Timeline for your button is created offering you the four standard states (Figure 9.14).

Figure 9.14 Flash creates four states for your new button.

Initially the button has only one empty keyframe in its 'up' state. Select this frame and then create some graphic on the Stage to represent the 'up state' of the button. It's useful to remember that the crosshair in the middle of the Stage gives you a fixed point of reference to work from.

For this example, we'll choose to place a filled circle as our basic button (Figure 9.15). Once that has been placed we click on Frame 2 and make it a keyframe (by right-clicking). For our 'over' state we can give its edge a stroked outline using the Ink Bottle tool. (Duplicating the previous keyframe means we can get our alignments sorted out.)

For the 'down' state we once again convert Frame 3 into a keyframe and this time 'paint out' the inside of the circle with a clear area.

The last 'hit' state doesn't worry about what colours are used. It is only to guide Flash as to which area of the Stage belongs to the button's area of influence. Some people feel comfortable having the entire 'hit' state depicted in some colour such as cyan so that they can immediately recognise it when they see it. For this example we'll once again fill the circle. The fact that the hit state is exactly the same size as the overall button helps the user in determining the button's area.

Once the button has been completed you need to return to movie editing mode. A copy of your button will be placed in the library and it is from here that you can place an instance of it on to your Stage area.

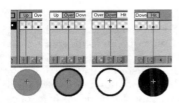

Figure 9.15 The four basic button shapes.

*Just as when you set frame actions, Flash by default switches off the option of allowing you to view the button states in editing mode. If it didn't, you would find great difficulty in repositioning them or working with them. But to switch off this default you do virtually the same as for frame actions. Go to your **Control** menu, but this time select **Enable Buttons**. However, it is usually best to test your buttons by going to **Control:Test Scene**.*

There is absolutely no reason why you should stick to the same shaped graphic for each of your button states. You could have, for instance, a square, a circle and a star for the three 'up', 'down' and 'over' states – just so long as your 'hit' state is large enough to cover the entire area of the three other states.

An easy way to ensure your 'hit' state is large enough is to **Edit:Copy** and **Edit:Paste in Place** each of the initial three states into the 'hit' keyframe. That way you can be sure that each of the different shapes is effectively recognised when you mouse-over the button. You could even use the **Modify:Curves:Expand Shape** by a pixel or two making the 'hit' area slightly bigger than is necessary so that the button is activated when the mouse cursor is near the actual button.

There is absolutely no reason why the 'hit' state of a button needs to be in the vicinity of the rest of the button, nor why there should be only one hot spot. You could have hot spots dotted around the Stage if you wanted to!

Interactivity with buttons

Now that we have learned the basics about creating buttons, they can be used for helping the user to interact with your movie. Apart from the normal 'up', 'down' and 'over' states, you can get Flash to react to these same mouse cursor events by completing certain actions. If you right-click on the button instance you will be able to bring up its **Properties** (Figure 9.16) and it's here, once again, that you can set what are known as **MouseEvent** actions.

Figure 9.16 Assigning actions to buttons from the Instance Properties dialog box.

As before, we click on the + button to add actions (see Figure 9.3); let's choose 'Go To'. This time Flash adds the lines:

```
On (Release)
Go to and Stop (1)
End On
```

All button actions are structured in this way. The 'On (MouseEvent)' and 'End On' lines enclose what Flash must do when the button is activated. You will recognise in Figure 9.17 the parameter settings that we can fill in for particular actions. They are very similar to those which we saw in Figure 9.10.

 If you want to add additional events within the 'On (MouseEvent)' and 'End On' tags, highlight the line above where you want to add an event and then click on the + button. The new action will be added immediately below this highlighted line.

Although Flash defaults to the 'On (Release)' command, you can just as easily set the action to occur on any of eight MouseEvent occurrences. As you can see in Figure 9.18, by clicking on the first line within the action list, a new parameter box appears on the right offering you a number of options.

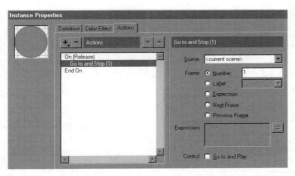

Figure 9.17 Setting action parameters is similar to the Frame Properties dialog box.

Figure 9.18 Change the value of 'MouseEvent' by clicking on the first line.

1. **Press**: occurs when the button is clicked downwards.

2. **Release**: occurs when the button is released after it has been clicked down, but only if the cursor is still in the button area. If the button is clicked and then the mouse dragged off the button before being let go, then the action will not happen.

3. **Release Outside**: is the opposite of Release, in that the mouse must be outside the button's area before being released after clicking, otherwise the action will not happen.

4. **Roll Over**: will occur any time that the mouse invades the button's hit area.

5. **Roll Out:** occurs whenever the mouse rolls out of the button's active area.

6. **Drag Over:** works when the user holds down the mouse within the button area, rolls the cursor outside of the active area and then returns within that area once more.

7. **Drag Out:** happens when the mouse button is pressed over the button, and the pointer is then moved out of the active area.

8. **Key Press:** occurs whenever the specified key is pressed. The user does not have to use the mouse for this event to occur, however, and the mouse cursor does not have to be anywhere near the button in question. Simply, the button must be 'visible' somewhere on the Stage.

We've seen that if you issue a command such as 'Go To' before specifying the mouse action, Flash defaults to 'On (Release)' as the specific action. You might find it more convenient first to select 'On MouseEvent' from the Action list, so that you can specify your action, and then further refine your action commands.

Buttons can get your movie to react in different ways, depending on whether, for instance, you click the button or move the cursor over the button, or even press a key on the keyboard.

When you assign actions from the action list as shown in Figure 9.18, there is no reason why you cannot stack them so that, for instance, you can issue one set of commands dependent on **On (Press)** and another one on **On (Roll Out)** and a third on **On (Key:X)** (Figure 9.19).

Figure 9.19 Multiple choice actions.

Buttons don't actually have to have any graphics on them at all. Instead you could use what are referred to as 'invisible buttons'. As long as the hit frame has content, then you can ask your users to click anywhere within an area of the screen to launch the next action. This might be useful if, for instance, you wanted to pause an interactive presentation and let your users resume play simply by clicking anywhere.

10

Sound

How Flash handles sounds

Importing sounds

Adding sounds to frames

Adding sounds to buttons

Sync settings

Streaming sounds

Making simple edits to your sound files

■ How Flash handles sounds

Just as the arrival of pictures on Web sites revolutionised the entire way in which the World Wide Web was used, and was the main reason that its use grew in such a spectacular fashion, the use of sound on Web sites is also becoming pervasive across the Internet.

Flash can handle sounds that have been recorded in WAV (.wav) format and these can be used either as one-off events (such as a click sound when a button is pressed) or as a streaming sound that, for instance, delivers background music as your movie progresses.

These two types of sound are handled differently by Flash and it is important to understand where the main differences lie:

- An **event** sound has to download completely before it can play. It will then keep on playing until instructed to stop.
- A **streaming** sound starts to play as soon as enough information has been downloaded for the first few frames. Thereafter the sound is synchronised to the Timeline as Flash forces the frames to keep pace with the sound. If the frames take too long to draw, Flash drops some of the frames in order to keep up.

■ Importing sounds

You import sounds in exactly the same way you would import bitmaps and other artwork. From the **File** menu choose **Import** and choose the format to read **WAV Sound (*.wav)** before selecting your particular sound (Figure 10.1).

 *You can import as many WAV files as you like in one go by holding down the **Ctrl** key as you select the different files.*

Flash imports the WAV files into its library for you to use as required. Remember, you can inspect the contents of your library by selecting **Window:Library** (or **Ctrl-L**) and in the preview window you will see the waveform for each selected sound file. Clicking on the Play button allows you to hear what the file sounds like (Figure 10.2).

Figure 10.1 Importing WAV files.

Figure 10.2 You can 'preview' your sound files directly in the Library window.

Although there is nothing to stop you adding sounds to graphics layers, you will find it easier to allocate separate layers to individual sounds and to keep these layers together so that you can easily find particular sounds when it's time to update or edit them.

Flash does not, of itself, group all sound layers together, but you can cheat by creating a mask layer and adding the sound layers as masked layers, thereby creating a hierarchy (Figure 10.3). Because there are no graphics to worry about in these layers, the fact that they are masked makes no difference to the playback of your sound files.

*You can see in Figure 10.3 that we have enlarged the height of the sound layers. By doing so it is possible to see more of the waveform of the sounds for better placing your graphics and action files. To enlarge a layer within your Timeline select **Modify:Layer** and set your layer height to 100% (normal), 200% or 300%.*

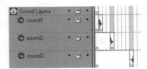

Figure 10.3 Add sounds layers as masked layers for easy identification.

■ Adding sounds to frames

You can assign any sound that is currently in your movie's library by dragging it to the Stage once you have selected, or created, a keyframe. It obviously doesn't matter where you drop the sound file on the Stage since the sound is 'invisible'; but you will see a sound symbol outline and Flash will attach that sound file to the keyframe you have selected.

Now, you can add a sound instance by dragging it from either the main sound library (**Libraries:Sounds**) if it is included in it, or from the movie's sound library (**Window:Library**), assuming it is already there. However, you can also add it by calling up the Frame Properties dialog box and selecting the **Sound** tab; you can then inspect the sound pop-up menu to select the sound from the movie's library (Figure 10.4).

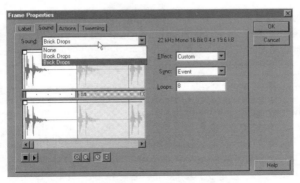

Figure 10.4 Selecting a sound from the Frame Properties dialog box.

We'll return to the other options in this dialog box in a short while.

■ Adding sounds to buttons

It can be very useful for your viewers to have sounds allocated to your buttons. Apart from adding a touch of reality, they can also help to highlight hot spots when the cursor is moved over them.

With your button visible on stage, **right-click** on it and choose **Edit** to open it up in Symbol Editing mode. Add a new layer in the Timeline and label it **Sounds**. We now want to assign two sounds to the button – one when the user's cursor hovers over it and another when the button is clicked.

First, then, you need to **Insert:Blank Keyframes** into both the **Over** and **Down** states. Then you assign sounds to each of these two keyframes in the way we have just described. You should see a Timeline similar to that shown in Figure 10.5.

Figure 10.5 Adding sounds to a button.

Once you are happy with the placing of the sounds, you can return to Movie Editing mode by clicking on the **Scene** button shown at the top left of Figure 10.5. Remember that you can only 'preview' the sounds by first selecting **Control:Enable Buttons**.

There is no reason why you cannot allocate sounds to the 'up' and 'hit' states of the button. In these cases, you would hear the sounds when you either rolled the cursor out of the button's area, or when you released the button within the active hit area respectively.

■ Sync settings

We saw in Figure 10.4 that there were some other drop-down menu boxes which were pertinent to the way that sounds played along the Timeline. If we begin by looking at the Sync drop-down menu, we can see there are four options (Figure 10.6):

1. Event
2. Start
3. Stop
4. Stream

Figure 10.6 Choosing a Sync setting.

By default, Flash sets a sound to play as an 'Event'. This means that the beginning of the sound is set to a particular keyframe, regardless of what is happening around it in the rest of the movie.

This can impact on your movie in two dramatic ways. For instance, as all the information to play an event sound is contained within a specific keyframe, Flash will pause to download all the sound information from that frame and only continue with the rest of the movie once it has finished. This means that you should only use short sounds as event sounds, otherwise your movie could become jerky as it stops and starts waiting for long sounds to download.

Another aspect of the 'Event' choice is that, were a sound to be longer than the overall length of the section of your movie in which it is contained, then it will keep on playing even after that section has come to an end. The way to stop this happening is to insert a Stop command.

Choose where you want your sound to stop and insert a blank keyframe. Although this has the effect of cutting off your view of the waveform in the Timeline, the sound will continue to play. However, if you now go to the Frame Properties dialog box for this blank keyframe and choose the **Sound** tab, you can specify in the Sync menu to stop the sound and also specify the name of the sound you want stopped (Figure 10.7).

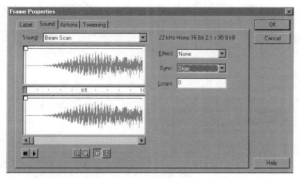

Figure 10.7 Issuing a Stop command.

To let you know a Stop command has been issued, Flash places a small square in the Timeline where the sound ends (Figure 10.8)

Figure 10.8 A Stop command is issued.

 *If you want to stop all sounds at a particular frame, use instead the **Stop All Sounds** instruction from the **Actions** menu of your Frame Properties dialog box.*

Adding two sounds simultaneously

Flash can play as many sounds simultaneously as you like. However, only one sound can be assigned to each keyframe, so this means that if you want two sounds to start at the same frame, then each must be assigned to a separate layer. (Remember, though, that the more sounds Flash has to download, the longer the pause will be at this particular frame.)

Alternatively, if you want one sound to start after the other but both sounds to be playing simultaneously, it is quite in order for the two sounds to be placed on the same layer, as long as they are not instructed to start in the same frame.

Start sounds

At first, it appears that **Start Sounds** has an almost identical behaviour pattern to **Event Sounds**. The sound is started when a specific keyframe is encountered.

The important difference, however, is that with a *Start* sound instruction, only one instance of this sound can play at any one time, whereas with an *Event* sound, you can have multiple instances of the same sound playing simultaneously.

This means that if, for instance, a movie is set to loop and the sound that kicks off in the first loop playback is still playing when this frame repeats, then:

- If the sound is an *Event* sound you will hear two instances of the sound playing simultaneously (but not necessarily in sync).
- If the sound is a *Start* sound, only the first instance will play, and there will be no repeat until such time as the first instance of the sound has stopped and the scene has looped again to hit the keyframe containing the sound.

We referred just now to scene looping. And just as a scene or movie can loop (when frame actions are set this way), so too can a sound be made to loop a specific number of times. If you look at Figure 10.4 you will see there is a dialog box in which you can specify the number of times a sound should loop.

■ Streaming sounds

Unlike Event sounds that must be completely downloaded before they can play, Streaming sounds start playing once only a fraction of the information has downloaded. By setting the **Sync** to **Stream**, Flash synchronises it with specific frames of your movie and plays the sound until either a new keyframe is encountered, or a Stop command is issued.

In Streaming Audio, Flash subdivides the sound into clips whose length is proportional to the overall frame rate. So, if the frame rate is set to the default of 12 frames per second, each clip of sound is created to last 1/12th of a second. Each of these subclips is timed to start with each new frame encountered, but if the sound is too fast for the images, Flash sacrifices some of the frames to keep up with the sounds. This could have the effect of making the movie look jerky, but that is simply one of the downsides to streaming audio against a fixed frame rate.

With streaming sounds, you can hear how the sound interacts with the different frames by 'scrubbing' along the Timeline. Drag the playhead across the Timeline and see how the sound peaks coincide with different aspects of the frame contents (see Figure 10.9).

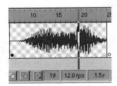

Figure 10.9 'Scrubbing' along the Timeline.

If the synchronisation is not to your liking, you can add or delete frames to improve the timing. This can be made simpler if you switch between different views in your Frame Properties dialog box (as shown in Figures 10.10 and 10.11).

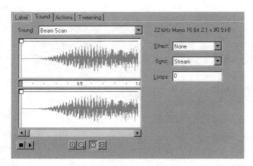

Figure 10.10 Time view of the sound sequence.

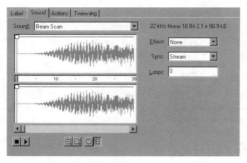

Figure 10.11 Frame view of the sound sequence.

By clicking on the **Seconds** and **Frames** view buttons at the bottom of the Frame Properties dialog box it is possible to deduce exactly how many frames you need to add or delete to make your sound file fit your frames sequence.

■ Making simple edits to your sound files

To a limited degree, Flash allows you to make superficial edits to your sound files. You can alter:

■ the start and end points of the sound;

- its volume; and
- the relationship between the left and right stereo channels.

(However, for any serious editing it is probably better to edit the sound files in programs specific to the task.)

To change the volume of sound files with Flash, you begin by opening up the **Sound** tab of the Frame Properties dialog box.

The **Effect** tab is where you can choose one of the following:

- None
- Left Channel
- Right Channel
- Fade Left to Right
- Fade Right to Left
- Fade In
- Fade Out
- Custom

As you can see in Figure 10.12, the volume levels of both right and left channels can be set by dragging the envelope handles up or down. Choose one of the cross-fade options, and the volume levels are set automatically.

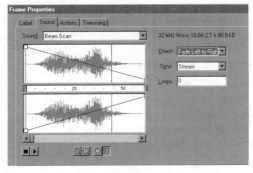

Figure 10.12 Setting a cross-fade from the Frame Properties dialog box.

You can add more handles by clicking on the waveform – to a maximum of eight per channel – and each can then be dragged up or down, left or right, to change the volume levels along the playback line of the sound file (Figure 10.13).

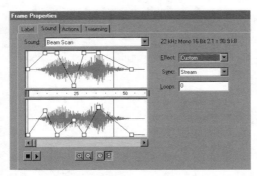

Figure 10.13 A sound file can contain up to eight handles for each channel.

To remove unwanted envelope handles you simply drag them from the window. To hear the resulting sound, click on the Play icon shown in the bottom left-hand corner of Figure 10.13.

 As we have already mentioned, Flash's sound editing is pretty basic, but it does allow for some simple effects. If you are likely to cut back the overall length of many of your sound files it may still be worth doing so in an external sound editing program since, although Flash can be set to ignore the start and end points of the sound, the overall file is still contained in the final Flash movie. This just takes up unnecessary space, making your final movie bigger than it needs to be.

11
Complex interactivity

∎ ∎

Expressions and variables

Other actions

Conditions

Re-using the same actions with Call

Incorporating Javascript with FS Command

Debugging and commenting out your movie

We've seen how Flash allows you to interact with your movies in a number of ways – not least through the use of actions sparked off by clicking buttons or the choice of specific items on menus. With the arrival of version 4, Macromedia introduced complex interactivity into Flash for the first time. It introduced variables and expressions, allowing the site designer to use formulaic interactivity that would test for certain conditions and carry out an action specific to the outcome of a particular test.

Using expressions and variables in Flash takes a little while to grasp. Many people find it much more difficult to come to grips with than other aspects of the design of a Flash production. However, we would strongly recommend working through the following pages, trying out the expressions for yourself and learning by experimentation. That way you should find that what appears daunting at first opens out a whole new vista for your site development and brings Flash into a realm of its own.

In short, you will wonder how you could ever have done without some of these wonderful additions to Flash!

■ Expressions and variables

So let's start by defining exactly what we mean by expressions and variables.

An *expression* is a type of formula made up of a mathematical combination of *variables*. Say you wanted to set a password made up from your birth date and another number set by the programmer. We could make it equivalent to the sum of the day of the month, the number of the month and the year in which you were born, plus the final number – 'X'.

So, if that birthday were 13 February 1981 and the extra number was 4, then the password would be $13 + 2 + 1981 + 4 = 2000$.

Put as a mathematical expression we could say *password = day + month + year + X*. Here, *day*, *month*, *year* and X are all variables.

Variables which can be added or amended by the viewer of the movie are called **concrete variables**. Variables that exist only in the inner workings of Flash, but over which the viewer has no control, are called **abstract variables**. So in the above example, *day*, *month* and *year* are concrete variables, whilst *X* is an abstract variable.

Concrete variable fields are added to a movie by selecting the Text icon in the toolbar and then clicking on the Text field modifier button (shown on the far right in Figure 11.1).

Figure 11.1 Selecting the Text field modifier.

Let's set up a very simple Flash scene that works out this password for us. Open up a new Flash document and select the Text tool, making sure the Text field modifier icon is also selected (Figure 11.1). Create a text box and then right-click on it; select **Properties**.

A dialog box similar to that shown in Figure 11.2 opens up. You will see that the first box is the variable, and this is where you give the text variable a name – in this case '*Day*'.

- The first of the check box options listed is to **draw a border** round your text field. As you want the viewer to be able to see this box before they start typing in their details, we tick the box to make it show up.

- The second check box is to **set a password** in case the user has to enter something to allow him or her to go any further with the interactivity. We'll leave it blank for now.

- The **multiline** entry allows the user to add as many lines of text as he or she likes, and to wrap that text to the width of the window. As we only want the user to enter a simple number this time we will again leave this blank. (By doing so, the next check box, Word Wrap, is greyed out.)

- We can **restrict** the user to a maximum number of characters in the next field. Days of the month can only be one or two characters long, so we have ticked the box and entered the number '2' here.

- It could well be that we want the user to know what we have entered into the text box, but we do not want the user to edit it; in which case the '**disable editing**' box is checked.

- If we choose to disable editing, we can also choose whether or not the text field can be **selected**, otherwise the check box is again greyed out.

- The **outlines** options allow you to choose whether you want to *save the font outlines* with the published movie, and if so you can choose to select only upper case, lower case, numbers and so on. Selecting your outline options carefully can reduce the overall file size of your published movie.

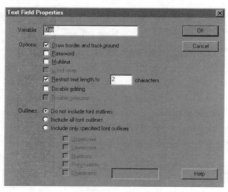

Figure 11.2 The Text Field Properties dialog box is where you specify your variable properties.

Having set the options for the first of our text fields, we can add similar fields for the *month*, *year* and – if we want – for the *X* number. With the latter, of course, we have chosen this particular number, so we have to disable editing and selection, just as we do when we add our final field, *password*.

It will also help if we put a text label beside each box so that when the user views the movie he or she knows which field is which (see Figure 11.3). Remember to deselect the Text field modifier icon when adding your labels.

Day of the month

Month

Year

'X' number   4

Password

Figure 11.3 Adding the text fields with their labels to the Stage. Note how the active (password) field has a little box in its bottom right-hand corner signifying it is an editable text field.

Having placed labels and text fields on the Stage, the next job is to specify the relationships between the different variable fields. Let's get Flash to generate our new password when we click on a button.

Figure 11.4 Making a selection from the Actions list.

Place an instance of a button on the Stage and double-click it to access its Instance Properties dialog box. From its Actions tab, click on the **+** icon to get a menu of actions and select **Set Variable** (Figure 11.4).

Flash inserts the Actions list to read:

```
On (Release)
Set Variable:  "="
End On
```

By filling in the details in the right hand panes (shown in Figure 11.5) Flash automatically constructs the expression Actions list in the left-hand pane. If we set our variable as *Password*, and add *Day + Month + Year + X* as our value, then when we click the button, Flash should make the password equal to this sum of the variables (Figure 11.6).

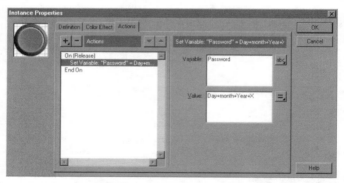

Figure 11.5 Here we set the variable 'Password' to equal the sum of the other fields.

The example we have just worked through is quite straightforward. Sometimes, however, creating complex expressions can be daunting; but Flash rides to the rescue once more by offering to help you create the expression via its **Expression Editor**. Instead of adding the sum of the variables to the Value box as we did just now, click instead on the **=** icon to the right of the Value box

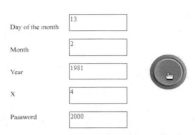

Figure 11.6 Testing the scene from the Control menu ensures the expression has been entered correctly.

shown in Figure 11.5 and select **Expression Editor**. Here (Figure 11.7) you can select from scrolling lists of operators and functions and Flash will automatically add the correct syntax of each that you choose to your expression.

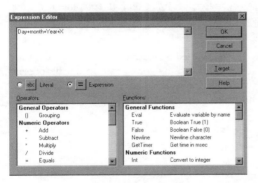

Figure 11.7 The Expression Editor helps you enter more complex expressions.

■ Other actions

Apart from using simple expressions, we saw in Figure 11.4 that there are plenty of other options that we can choose from our Actions list.

Loading new files into your movie

The Actions menu has a couple of entries that allow you to load new files in to your movie or Web site:

- **Get URL** is used to load a file into your browser window when the Flash file is played using a browser.
- **Load Movie** loads new movie files on top of your current movie so that the latter is either replaced by the former, or complemented by another animation layer.

 URL is short for Uniform Resource Locator, which is a way of specifying a Web site address. An absolute URL gives information about the server on which the Web site is located, the path to the Web site itself and the name of the file being called. A relative URL, on the other hand, describes the address of the file relative to the current page being displayed. When testing your movies on your computer, relative URLs allow you to specify files on your computer in relation to others rather than making you get on to the Internet to find an absolute address.

In Figure 11.8, we have entered a relative URL – *newmovie.swf* – which can be found in the same root position as the present movie. Notice how the URL is defined as a text string (shown by the **abc** icon) rather than as a numeric variable.

Figure 11.8 Entering a Get URL action.

The Window drop-down menu gives four choices:

1. **_blank** (shown) forces the new URL to be loaded into a new window.
2. **_self** specifies the current frame in the current window.
3. **_parent** loads the URL into the current frame's parent.
4. **_top** ensures the URL is loaded into the top-level frame within the current window.

Finally you can determine whether you want Flash to **GET** or **POST** variables (or not to pass any at all) to your URL address. This is useful if you need to send variables to a CGI script which generates a .swf file as its CGI output. (We'll get more familiar with Shockwave – .swf – file formats in the next chapter.) If you aren't familiar with CGI commands you are probably best leaving this option set to *Don't Send*.

*The Get URL action command can also be used to send information in an email. In the parameters side of the Actions list, enter **mailto:address** where 'address' is the email address of the person you wish to email. (So, to email us you could insert **mailto:info@top-spin-group.com**.) If you have two fields – one whose variable value is 'body' and the other 'subject' – then the contents of 'subject' will be inserted into your email message subject line, and the contents of 'body' will be inserted into the email body text.*

To test your Get URL action, go to the **File** menu and select **Publish Preview:HTML**. Your movie is exported as a .swf file, and an HTML file is created which embeds the .swf file; this HTML file is then opened up in the browser of your choice. Now when you click your button you should see the new URL page loaded into the frame specified in your Window drop-down menu.

To load a new movie choose the option **Load/Unload Movie** from the Actions menu (Figure 11.4). This action is used to play new movies without closing down the Flash player. For instance, if you wanted to play a series of banner adverts you could use a Load Movie action at the end of one .swf file to load the next movie sequentially. Alternatively, if you wanted to allow the user to choose from several .swf files you could build an interactive branch to take the user to one .swf file or another depending on which button the user clicked.

In the resulting Load Movie parameters box (Figure 11.9) you first of all choose the action to perform. The choice is:

1. Load movie into location
2. Unload movie from location
3. Load variables into location

Again, the third option here requires you to understand the use of CGI scripts. If you don't, then ignore this option. If the user were to submit an order form you could use this option to display a confirmation order number sent from a file on your remote server.

Figure 11.9 The Load Movie parameters box.

Unlike the Get URL action above, we are offered the choice of setting the level or target for this action. Let's consider the Level setting first of all. By default, the movie that you are currently in is always in Level 0. Movies in levels higher than the present one are always loaded on top; so if – as in Figure 11.9 – we specify Level 1, we are instructing Flash to play the new movie on top of the present one. That means that if the new movie is located above the present one, it will obscure whatever is beneath it.

You can test the Load Movie action by choosing **Test Movie** from your **Control** menu.

Tell Target

Flash allows you to control a different movie clip from the one that is playing by using the action *Tell Target*. Its main use is in navigation where, by clicking on a button, you can instruct Flash to jump to a particular frame within a movie clip, or to start a movie clip somewhere else on the Stage.

For this example we will use one of the movie clips provided in Flash's library – the biplane – and two instances of any of the buttons. We will get one of the buttons to stop the action of the plane's propeller, and the other button to start it again.

In order to be able to instruct the buttons to carry out instructions on a particular movie clip, we have to give that clip a name. It is no good assuming that Flash can find the particular instance of the biplane because there may be more than one instance of each clip.

On the Stage, select the instance of the biplane by right-clicking on it and then select **Properties**. The Instance Properties dialog box will appear as in Figure 11.10.

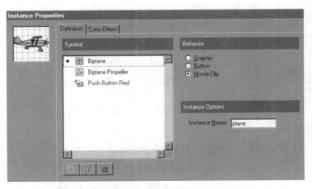

Figure 11.10 The Instance Properties dialog box.

In the lower right-hand corner is an empty text field where we give this movie instance a unique name. We'll call it 'plane'. By so doing, we can direct any button to target this particular instance of the movie clip, irrespective of how often the clip appears in our final movie.

Having given a unique identifier to the movie clip we are able to start giving instructions to the buttons to perform specific actions. On the stage we place two button instances and label one *Play* and the other *Stop*.

Double-click on the **Stop** button to bring up its Instance Properties dialog box and click on the **Actions** tab. By using the **Add** menu we select **Tell Target** and Flash adds the following text to the actions list:

```
On (Release)
Begin Tell Target ("")
End Tell Target
End On
```

We now have to point the action to the correct movie clip. (As we only have one clip, this is easy!) As you can see in Figure 11.11, one can either double-click on the list of movie clips listed in the top right frame, or type in the target's name with a forward slash preceding it. Either way, Flash adds */plane* in the Tell Target instruction on the left.

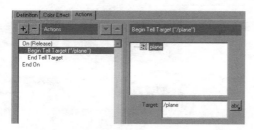

Figure 11.11 Here we instruct Flash to associate the plane clip with this particular button.

With `Begin Tell Target ("/plane")` selected, we now call up the Actions menu again and choose **Stop**. Again, Flash updates the Actions List (Figure 11.12).

Figure 11.12 The complete Actions list for the Stop button.

We now do exactly the same for the second (play) button, but instead of adding *Stop* as our last action, we add *Play*.

Now to see the Tell Target commands in action, we have to go to the **Control** menu and select **Test Movie**. Clicking on the **Stop** button stops the plane's propeller from rotating. The **Play** button starts it once again.

Figure 11.13 The Stop and Play buttons control the propeller of the plane.

*It is possible to specify a target movie clip using expressions rather than hierarchical addresses. For example, you could specify that a movie represented by the variable in a button be targeted. If the variable were called **Buttonvariable**, for example, then you could target "/"&Buttonvariable as your expression.*

Say you wanted the press of a button to stop movie clip A and start movie clip B from Frame number 20. Your action could read something like:

```
On (Press)
Begin Tell Target ("/A")
Stop
End Tell Target
End On
On (Release)
Begin Tell Target ("/B")
Go to and Play (20)
End Tell Target
Go to Next Frame
End On
```

▪ Conditions

Referring back to Figure 11.4, you will see that there are three conditional actions listed:

1. If frame is loaded
2. If
3. Loop

These allow you to test for the verity of statements or check whether a certain condition has been met, and to act according to the result.

If Frame is Loaded

The first condition – *If frame is loaded* – speaks for itself. This is useful, for example, if you want to test whether data has been downloaded to the user's computer before starting playback of a particular scene. If there is a great deal of animation you will get much smoother animation if the sequence has entirely down-loaded first, rather than relying on the download to finish when the beginning is already playing. So, to keep your user amused while the rest of the movie clip is downloading you could have a teaser movie that repeats over and over again until the signal is given that the rest of the movie has downloaded.

It is difficult to try out an example of this action on your computer, since the download time is likely to be too fast for you to see the delay in action. Flash does try to simulate the streaming of movies (in your Flash Player go to **Control:Show Streaming** – Figure 11.14) but it is still difficult to see the full effect. Suffice it to say that there are thousands of examples of such an action on the World Wide Web where a splash screen appears and which – at first glance – might appear to serve little useful purpose except to deny access to the main body of the site. In reality it's all rather like the proverbial swan on water: serene on top, but feverish activity underneath. Whilst the splash screen diverts your attention, the movie is loading on to your computer out of sight until the condition is met to allow you access to it.

Figure 11.14 Show Streaming gives you an idea of the movie download.

Testing for a downloaded movie clip is easy enough. In your Actions dialog box select **If Frame is Loaded** and in the parameters section on the right-hand side of the box enter the scene (if different from the current one) and the frame number if you don't want to start at the beginning of the clip.

Now you need to tell Flash what to do once the frame has loaded. We might, for instance, suggest that if Frame 100 has been loaded the movie can start playing from Frame 15. So, with the *If Frame is Loaded* statement selected, we now add another action – in this case **Go To and Play** – and in the parameters box give the frame number – 15 (see Figure 11.15).

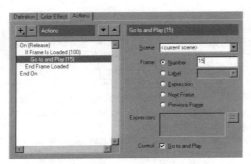

Figure 11.15 Defining If Frame is Loaded actions.

Looping an animation

Having created the conditional action to test if a frame has downloaded, it is likely you will want to loop your teaser animation until such time as the download is complete. The most straightforward way of doing this is to insert a **Go To** command at the end of your animation to instruct the clip to return to the first frame of the animation. That way the clip repeats over and over again. If you then insert your *If Frame is Loaded* conditions throughout the movie clip you can instruct Flash to start the next movie clip once the condition has been met.

Looping has other uses, too. Using a conditional loop, you can test if certain conditions are met and only when they are should Flash perform the next action.

For instance, you could set a variable – index – to equal 1. Every time the loop instructions are carried out, the index variable increases by 1. Only when the index has a value equal to or greater than 10 will the loop condition be met and Flash can then move on to the next instruction. Figure 11.16 shows such a loop command.

Figure 11.16 Using a Loop action to test for a condition.

If...Else

Just as Loop statements can test for certain actions, so too can **If** and **If...Else** statements. Using *If* you can choose to run an action only when a certain condition exists. You can use the logical operators offered by the Expression Editor, if you wish, to help you construct your *If* statements. You can also nest a number of *If...Else* statements to give alternative instructions if one condition is not met, but another is.

For example we could nest such statements so that a movie is played depending on which season of the year it currently is:

```
If (month eq "March" or "April" or "May")
Go to and Play ("Spring.swf",1)
Else if (month eq "June" or "July" or
  "August")
Go to and Play ("Summer.swf",1)
Else if (month eq "September" or "October"
  or "November")
Go to and Play (Autumn.swf",1)
Else if (month eq "December" or "January"
  or "February")
Go to and Play ("Winter.swf",1)
End If
```

■ Re-using the same actions with Call

Quite often you may wish to use the same actions, but assigned to different buttons or frames. Of course, you could copy and paste the same statements between buttons and frames; but a neater way is to assign an action to a specific frame, and then use the **Call** statement to run that action.

You could, for instance, create a library of actions by making a movie made up of actions assigned to separate frames. Each frame could then be labelled to make it easier to identify the frame you wish to call, although Flash is capable of being told to Call a specific frame number.

If Flash cannot find the called frame – perhaps the movie has not yet downloaded to your computer – it simply ignores the Call statement. You could, of course, add an 'If Frame is Loaded' statement to test if your Call instruction can be carried out successfully.

■ Incorporating Javascript with FS Command

Flash allows you to communicate with the browser hosting the Flash player, or the stand-alone projector. Using the **FS Command** statement, a message can be sent from Flash to the browser or projector, for instance, to cause the movie to fill the screen, or to hide the menu bar.

Writing Javascript routines is beyond the scope of this book, but the FS Command statement can be used for opening message dialog boxes in a browser, or causing a projector movie to fill the entire screen (see Figure 11.17).

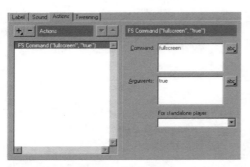

Figure 11.17 FS Command can be used to cause the projector to fill the screen.

■ Debugging and commenting out your movie

The problem with creating highly interactive movies is that the more complicated they get, the more likely it is that you will 'lose the plot' when it comes to making changes or corrections.

It is best when creating complex movies to test the actions continually as you go along. You can add comments, or explanatory notes, at any stage in the proceedings so that when you come to revisit a particular section at a later date it is immediately clear what each action is meant to do (Figure 11.18).

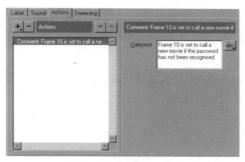

Figure 11.18 Adding comments helps you keep track of what is going on.

 It can be useful when testing a scene or a movie to get a list of all the existing variables or objects which you can do by going to **Control:List Objects** *or* **Control:List Variables**.

You can go further, however, by getting Flash to display information about what is going on when testing your movies. By using the **Trace** command, comments that you type into the Trace action's message parameter will appear in a new window as the action is carried out (Figure 11.19).

These comments will only appear when playing your movies in **Control:Test Movie** or **Control:Test Scene** modes; they will not appear, naturally, in your final published movie.

Figure 11.19 Using Trace to keep track of what is going on.

12
Publishing your movies

■ ■

OK. We've created our Flash masterpiece and have tested it out using the Test Movie functions incorporated into our editor. The time has now come to publish our Flash movie to allow others to use it.

Flash files can be viewed in a number of different ways, but the basis for everything is the Flash Player Format – or .swf file. This format is the only one that supports all the functions that we have experimented with in creating our Flash project; however, you can export movies into 'lesser' formats such as bitmapped images, animated images, vector files and so on. They can also be viewed as stand-alone 'projector' files. We'll return to all of these shortly.

Up to now we have been able to save our working files as Flash Movie (.fla) files, and it is important to understand the difference between these and the Player format (.swf) files. The former can be thought of as the development file standard. As we develop the movie, everything we create is saved in an all-encompassing Flash Movie file format which we can return to in order to edit or change settings at any time.

The published Player format file can be set to prohibit editing by anyone else, stopping others from exploring its inner workings.

■ Optimising playback

Perversely, before we start to export our movies, let's just pause for a moment to consider the all-important question of quality versus quantity. Naturally we want the final movie to be in as high a quality as possible. But, especially if the movie is to be viewed over the Web, there is a price to pay for higher quality, and that is longer download times.

All Web developers know that a compromise has to be struck between the quality and size of image files and the time it takes to download that file. That compromise is all the more important in Flash since not only is the download time important so as not to keep your users waiting too long, but if you are using streaming video, the last thing you want is for the movie to stop and start as large chunks of animation try to squeeze down the narrow tube of available bandwidth.

There are many things that affect the overall file size of your final movie. For instance:

- a large number of bitmapped images
- lots of keyframes
- sounds
- embedded fonts
- gradients instead of plain fills
- using individual graphic objects instead of symbols or groups

However, Flash does not leave you to fend for yourself. It can simulate streaming of both video and audio and graphs your bandwidth so you can see at a glance which frames are likely to cause problems. The key to this help can be found when you test your movie (**Control:Test Movie**).

The Control menu of the Flash Player (*not* the Editor) has some new options (Figure 12.1) which allow you to set the simulated download speed of your modem. You can see that the three most common modem speeds of 14.4, 28.8 and 56.6 Kbps are listed, but you can also set your modem to whatever download speed you wish to simulate.

Figure 12.1 Setting your simulated download speed.

Having set the simulated speed, you now need to go to your **View** menu and select **Bandwidth Profiler**. At the top of the screen Flash now presents you with a graph which shows how much information is being transmitted along the Timeline of your movie (Figure 12.2), each bar representing the amount of data in each frame. We've deliberately set our modem rate to 14.4 Kbps for this example and you will see how a number of frames just nudge over the bottom line (which is coloured red). This warns us that at this particular modem speed these particular frames may cause the movie to pause while they download. (Had we set the modem speed to 28.8 Kbps or above, none of these frames except for the first would have breached the bottom line, in which case our download should proceed with no hold-ups.)

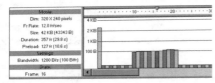

Figure 12.2 At this modem speed setting we may experience some pauses.

If we click on one of the bars, information about that particular frame, as well as about the movie in general, appear on the left-hand side.

Flash also shows how the movie will stream if we choose **View:Streaming Graph** from the player menu line. Each of the alternate bars of light and dark grey reflect the time taken to download that particular sector of information. When a frame contains very little information, you may well see several bars in a single time unit (as in the right-hand end of Figure 12.3).

*Flash can generate a printed report of the amount of information contained in your finished movie. When publishing the movie (see below) tick the box marked **Generate size report** under the Flash tab of the **Publish Settings** dialog box..*

Figure 12.3 In Streaming mode the width of the bar indicates how long it takes to download.

■ Publishing your movies for use on the Web

Flash's **Publish** command is used to create all the files necessary to view your Flash project file, even if the end user does not have a Flash Player to view the finished file. As well as preparing a Flash Player (.swf) file, Publish can also create alternative image formats for use on the Web in the event that the Flash Player is not available (such as GIF, JPEG, PNG and QuickTime). All the HTML code necessary to embed the finished file within a Web document is created automatically and Publish can also generate stand-alone projectors for both PCs and Macintosh systems.

When deciding on the formats that you wish Flash to generate you need to access the **Publish Settings** dialog box from the **File** menu (Figure 12.4). This allows you to publish in up to seven different formats as well as to create the necessary HTML code for displaying the finished files in a browser.

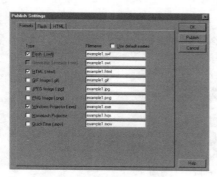

Figure 12.4 Selecting the Publish settings.

Having chosen your preferred formats, you can instruct Flash to publish your movie by clicking on the **Publish** button on the top right corner of the dialog box, or by going to the **File** menu at a later time and selecting **Publish**. The published files are all stored in the same directory location as the original movie.

 *By default, Flash names your published files by adding the appropriate extension to the current file name. If you want to give them another name you should first deselect the **Use default names** check box shown in Figure 12.4.*

■ Publishing your movies as stand-alone Flash Player files

As well as allowing you to publish your movies for use on the Web, or in a browser, Flash can also create stand-alone player applications.

First you need to select your Publish Settings as described above and make sure that the **Flash (.swf)** check box (as shown in Figure 12.4) is ticked.

The next tab in the Publish Settings dialog box is labelled **Flash**. Open this dialog box and you should see a list of options as shown in Figure 12.5.

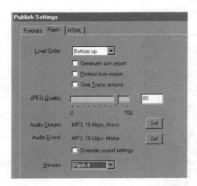

Figure 12.5 Setting options for your Flash Player file.

These options can be explained as follows:

- **Load Order** This affects the download of the first frame. When a slow network or modem is being used, Flash draws individual layers in the order set by this option. With the choice set to *Bottom up*, Flash begins to draw the lowest levels first.

- **Generate size report** As described above, this option generates a printed report about the size of your movie.

- **Protect from import** By ticking here you can prevent others from importing your movie back into a Flash editor.

- **Omit Trace actions** Trace comments add to the final size of your published movie file. Click here to remove them completely.

- **JPEG Quality** The JPEG format is what is known as a lossy compression file. The more you compress your JPEG image, the worse is its quality. By moving the JPEG Quality slider (or by entering a specific value) you can determine the amount of compression you want for your JPEG images. A high figure gives the best quality; a low one optimises the download time.

- **Audio Stream and Audio Event** Use these buttons to override the rate and compression levels for both streaming and event sounds (see Figure 12.6). Obviously for these settings to work there have to be sounds present in your movie! The compression pop-up menu gives you three choices: **ADPCM** is used for short event sounds. You can choose how much compression to apply to these sounds: 5-bit is the best quality option. **MP3** is used when you have longer streaming sounds and you can again determine its quality settings. At settings lower than 20 Kbps all sounds are played in mono, regardless of whether or not there was stereo content to begin with. A **Raw** setting causes no sound compression to be applied.

- **Override sound settings** The above settings will defer to your original choice of sound compression unless this check box is ticked. This could be useful if you wanted to create two versions of your movie: one lower quality one for Web use and another higher quality stand-alone version.

- **Version** To maintain backwards compatibility you can pub-lish your work as older Flash version movies. However, if you choose Flash 3 you will lose Flash 4-only features such as user-editable text and some interactive functions. Publishing as a Flash 2 movie will also cause you to lose your trans-parency options. There can surely be no reason why you would want to publish as a Flash 1 (Future Splash) file.

Figure 12.6 The Sound Settings dialog box.

▪ HTML Publishing

In order to play a Flash movie in a Web browser it is necessary to create the code to embed the .swf file into the HTML document.

By filling in blanks in a template depending on your choice of options, Flash can do a whole load of clever things such as detect-ing whether the browser used is capable of playing Flash movies and automatically downloading a player from the Web if necessary.

The HTML options are set using the **Publish Settings** choice in your **File** menu and selecting the tab marked **HTML** (see Figure 12.7).

These options are discussed below:

- **Template** You can choose from the drop-down menu one of a number of templates to use in creating your HTML file. The simplest template to use is the one called *Flash Only (Default)*. This only allows users who have browsers equipped with the Flash Player to see your movie. Other viewers will be unable to see it. Some of the other template choices, however, create HTML code that displays alternative images if the Flash Player is not present. To find out what each template offers, click on the **Info...** button to the right of the menu after you have made a selection.

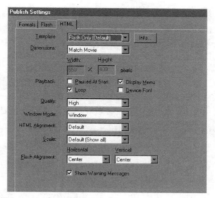

Figure 12.7 Setting your HTML options.

- **Dimensions** This option is used to determine the size of your final movie when played in the browser. The default is **Match Movie** which sets the dimensions to those of the movie itself; but you can also choose to size the movie as an exact number of pixels wide and high, or as a percentage of the browser window.

- **Playback** You are offered four choices to determine how the user views the final movie:

  Paused At Start requires the user to begin the movie manually – most probably by clicking a button or by choosing *Play* from the shortcut menu.

  Loop causes the movie to repeat when it reaches the last frame.

  Display Menu makes a shortcut menu available to users who right-click on the movie. If switched off, right-clicking will give information only about the Flash Player.

  Device Font substitutes anti-aliased system fonts for fonts that are not installed on the user's computer. This can speed up playback, but it works only on Windows systems; so if your movie is to be played on other platforms such as a Mac or Unix, you should leave this unselected.

- **Quality** This setting allows you to balance quality against the speed of playback.

Low switches anti-aliasing off permanently.

Autolow allows Flash to switch on anti-aliasing if it finds that your computer can handle the downloading of individual frames.

Autohigh assumes that anti-aliasing should be turned on unless the user's computer is unable to keep up with frame downloads.

High gives priority to appearance over playback speed. With no animation, bitmaps are smoothed; otherwise they are not.

Best smoothes all bitmaps and anti-aliasing is always switched on.

- **Window Mode** Windows users can allow your movie's transparency options to permit other elements to move behind the movie using Dynamic HTML and to either be hidden by the movie (**Opaque** setting) or show through (**Transparent Windowless**). This option is not available for users of other operating systems and Windows users must be using Internet Explorer v4 or above with the Flash Active X control.

- **HTML Alignment** You can specify whether you want your movie aligned within the browser window in the centre, left, right, top or bottom.

- **Scale** If you specify width and height settings which are different from the movie's original size, you can determine whether Flash resizes the movie keeping the aspect ratio of the original, or whether it stretches either or both sides of the movie to be an exact fit within the browser frame.

- **Flash Alignment** These settings determine how the movie is placed within its own window.

- **Show Warning Messages** Flash can display a warning if there are any conflicts in the tag settings.

■ Displaying alternative images

Quite often on the Web there will be people browsing who don't want to go to the bother of downloading a plug-in if their browser does not already support that standard. In such cases Flash can substitute animated or still images so that your viewer is not forced to look at a blank screen, or part of screen.

GIF images

If you have simple Web animations, you could, for instance, substitute animated GIF files which might take longer to download than the original Flash file, but would at least offer something to see. For this you need to select the option **Flash 4 with Image** from the template drop-down menu.

In your Publish Settings dialog box, check the tick box marked **GIF** (see Figure 12.4). A new tab appears at the top of the box marked GIF which you should now open (Figure 12.8). Once again, there are a number of options you can choose for your GIF file.

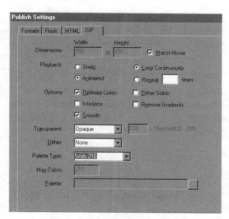

Figure 12.8 The GIF settings in the Publish Settings dialog box.

- **Dimensions** You can choose to have the GIF file the same size as the movie, or to determine the width and height of the image.

- **Playback** You can choose whether you want a single static image to be substituted, or the entire animation exported as an animated GIF. If the latter, you can then determine how many times it should loop through its playback.

- **Options** Here you can specify a number of options affecting the appearance of the GIF:

  Optimize colors removes unused colours from the colour table, thereby reducing the file size.

  Smooth enables or disables anti-aliasing.

  Interlace allows the exported GIF file to display incrementally rather than making the user wait for the entire image to downloaded before being able to view it.

  Dither Solids applies dithering to solids as well as gradients, giving a seemingly larger palette than the Web-safe palette of 216 colours would otherwise allow.

  Remove Gradients converts all gradient fills to solid fills, reducing file size and improving the colour since GIF gradients are often poor in quality due to the low number of available colours.

- **Transparent** Determines whether the background appears transparent or opaque, or whether colours below an Alpha threshold appear transparent. This threshold can be given any number between 0 and 255. It is often a good idea to experiment with this setting.

- **Dither** Here you can specify which type of dithering, if any, you wish Flash to perform in order to approximate to all the colours with only a limited colour palette. **Ordered** provides the best dithering for the least possible file size increase. **Diffusion** creates the best dithering irrespective of file size.

- **Palette Type** You can specify whether to use the Web-safe palette or customise the palette to your own specifications. The latter option often results in larger file sizes.

- **Max colors** If you select **Adaptive** or **Web Snap** options as your palette type, you can determine the maximum number of colours to be used in your GIF file.

JPEG and PNG images and QuickTime movies

Just as the GIF tab gives you a selection of options to choose from, so too do the JPEG and PNG tabs in the Publish Settings dialog box. The options are very similar, and therefore it should not be necessary to go through each of the settings again.

Suffice it to say, however, that whereas GIF files are ideal for line art drawings where there are large amounts of block colour, JPEGs are better for photographs and images that include gradients. In addition, the former are normally limited to 216 colours whereas JPEG files use the whole 16-million-colour palette.

PNG files can also support transparency (Alpha channels) but at the time of writing their use is not widespread on the World Wide Web.

QuickTime movies can be recognised both by Windows and Macintosh systems. Flash 4 creates QuickTime 4 format movies and these can recognise Flash's interactive features.

■ Projectors

For those who will view your movies without using a browser, Flash can create self-contained movie files which play without the aid of external programs. Projector files are self-sufficient in that they contain everything needed to replay a Flash movie.

 You can create projector files for both Windows and Macintosh operating systems, but Macintosh users need to convert the files using a program such as BinHex or Stuffit.

To create a projector file for Windows or Mac simply tick the check box(es) in the Publish Settings dialog box. There are no options to select for projector files, but Flash creates an .exe file for Windows use or a .hqx file for Mac users (Figure 12.9).

example1.exe   example1.hqx

Figure 12.9 Windows and Mac projector files.

■ Other image formats

As well as exporting Flash movies as JPEG, GIF and PNG images, you can also export individual frames as:

- EPS (Encapsulated PostScript)
- AI (Illustrator)
- PICT (Mac PICT)
- BMP (Windows Bitmap)
- WMF (Windows Metafile)
- EMF (Enhanced Metafile)
- DXF (Autocad DXF)

You can achieve any of these exports by going to the **File** menu and selecting **Export Image**. Alternatively, to export the movie as a sequence of frames, go to **File:Export Movie**. In addition to the above formats you can also export to

- AVI (Windows Audio Visual)
- WAV (WAV audio)

■ Printing from Flash

Flash allows you to print out individual frames or a number of frames together as a storyboard layout. However, you can only do this from the editor (.swa) file, not from the finished .swf file unless you do so from within a browser hosting the Flash Player movie file (and then only from the frame that is currently being shown).

From the **File** menu of the editor, choose **Page Setup** to determine page size, margins and whether you want the printer to print in portrait or landscape mode (Figure 12.10).

Figure 12.10 The Page Setup menu.

In the layout boxes you can choose whether you want to print out just the first frame or a selection of frames. If the latter, you should select **All frames** (Figure 12.11) and then choose which pages you wish to print in the **Print** dialog box (Figure 12.12).

Figure 12.11 Choose to print all frames or the first frame only.

The last drop-down menu allows you to specify whether you print out individual frames as single pages or as storyboard layouts (Figure 12.13).

Figure 12.12 Determine which pages you want to print out from your Print dialog box.

Figure 12.13 From this menu you can choose to print as individual pages or in a storyboard layout.

 *You can choose to print each frame number underneath their individual thumbnail images by selecting the **Label** check box in Page Setup when you choose one of the Storyboard options (Figure 12.14).*

Figure 12.14 You can choose to label frames when printing out a storyboard.

■ Conclusion

Now that you have reached the end of this book you are only at the beginning of discovering the many and varied things you can do with Flash 4. Some of the tasks may look daunting at first, but experimentation really does make for familiarity, and we cannot over-emphasise how versatile and essential this package is for anyone wishing to create first-rate dynamic Web sites and interactive movies.

Good luck in your creativity. The (animated) ball is now in your court!

Index